The Auditor's Report

WITH CASES
AND ILLUSTRATIONS

J. HERMAN BRASSEAUX, Ph.D., C.P.A.
Professor of Accounting and Chairman
Department of Accounting
Louisiana State University in New Orleans

FRANCIS L. MILES, B.B.A., C.P.A.
Audit Partner
Arthur Andersen & Co.
New Orleans, Louisiana

Published by

A48

SOUTH-WESTERN PUBLISHING CO.

Cincinnati   Chicago   Dallas   New Rochelle, N.Y.   Burlingame, Calif.   Brighton, England

23456K76543

Printed in the United States of America

Preface

This book provides a complete set of materials for teaching a sorely neglected area, the auditor's report. All facets of the auditor's report are explored with the greatest emphasis being placed on cases taken from actual situations. The focal point in each of the cases is the complex decision process in which the auditor engages in preparing the audit report. However, the cases also focus on the underlying reasons for the reporting problems; these are the variances from generally accepted auditing standards and from generally accepted accounting principles.

For the student, this book will add a necessary ingredient to the basic auditing course by providing materials for an intensive treatment of the reporting process. For the advanced auditing course or the graduate auditing course, the cases can provide a wealth of real-world situations that will further the student's understanding of and enhance his ability to deal with the audit report decision process.

For the business community, this book fulfills a vital need of public accounting firms in conducting in-house courses for their auditing staff; in addition, those corporate financial executives who work directly with the auditor in the preparation of financial statements and the related auditor's report will find these materials helpful in fulfilling their responsibilities.

Other features of the book include a comprehensive selection of illustrations of the auditor's report, a guide to the sequence of steps the auditor should follow in drafting his report, and a chapter discussing the auditor's legal responsibilities.

Except for the actual cases dealing with the auditor's legal responsibilities, the situations described in the cases have been drawn for the most part from experiences shown by the files of public accounting firms and by published annual reports. The cases taken from the files of public accounting firms have been modified where necessary to mask the identity of the companies; accordingly, except for Cases No. 23, 39, 40, and 41, all names are fictitious and are not intended to refer to real firms or individuals.

The authors wish to express their appreciation to Alexander N. Davidson, who served as special editor, for his many valuable suggestions in the preparation of this book.

J. Herman Brasseaux
Francis L. Miles

Contents

Introduction

It's Friday, February 5, 1971. George Brown, an audit partner in a national firm of Certified Public Accountants, is working late in his firm's offices in downtown San Francisco. In front of him are the working papers on the Bixby Manufacturing Company audit for the year ended December 31, 1970. Before starting on the first working draft of the auditor's report, George glances at the calendar and recalls that the Bixby report is due on February 23. At the same time, he is reminded of three other audit engagements that are due for completion in early March. Turning back to the Bixby audit report, George ponders and resolves several theory problems relating to the application of auditing standards and to the conformity of the financial statements with generally accepted accounting principles. However, he faces one last major unresolved issue: the use of an unacceptable accounting procedure by Bixby Manufacturing. George recalls vividly the discussion he and the senior staffman in charge of the Bixby audit had with the president of Bixby Manufacturing. The president insists that all accounting procedures used by Bixby were completely proper.

If you were George Brown, how would you prepare the auditor's report on this company? This decision is what this book is all about.

Purpose of the Book

The materials in this book are designed to assist the reader in developing skill in the audit decision process and in writing the auditor's report. In order to provide realistic, decision-oriented settings, cases have been drawn in most instances from actual experiences of independent public accounting firms. In most of the cases, the reader is provided with the audit evidence which has been assembled, and he is called upon to evaluate the evidence and make a decision as to the appropriate audit report to be issued under the circumstances. The reader thus receives experience in audit decision-making and in writing the auditor's report.

In an audit, the auditor must perform an examination in accordance with generally accepted auditing standards and make an assessment as to the fairness of the client's financial statements in relation to generally accepted accounting principles. Accordingly, in each of the cases in the book the focal issue involves an evaluation of accounting principles and practices or the application of auditing standards. Thus, the reader should gain skill in relating his knowledge of accounting principles and practices and auditing standards to simulated factual situations.

Authoritative Sources of Accounting Principles and Auditing Standards

The cases in this book dealing with departures from the standard short-form report have been arranged to correspond with the order in which they are discussed in Chapter 10 of *Statements on Auditing Procedure No. 33* (hereafter referred to as Statement No. 33), issued by the American Institute of Certified Public Accountants (hereafter referred to as the Institute). Statement No. 33 is the auditing profession's most authoritative guide to auditing standards and their application. Statement No. 33 and subsequent statements should be utilized by the reader in developing solutions to the cases. For an authoritative guide to accounting principles and practices, the student is referred to the *APB Accounting Principles* issued by the Institute.

Organization of the Book

The first chapter of this book provides background information on the auditor's report. A brief historical development of the form of the standard short-form report is given. To aid the reader in drafting proposed solutions to the various cases, a comprehensive selection of model auditor's reports is included. These model audit reports illustrate (a) the standard short-form report, (b) departures from the standard short-form report, (c) circumstances requiring a departure from the standard short-form report, and (d) special reports. In addition, a useful guide to the preparation of the auditor's report is provided.

Chapter 2 contains four groupings of cases relating to departures from the standard short-form report: (a) limitations in scope of examination; (b) fairness of presentation of financial statements; (c) consistency of application of accounting principles; and (d) existence of unusual uncertainties in financial statements.

Chapter 3 contains cases which illustrate the auditor's problems in preparing special reports and finally, because the auditor's legal responsibility is receiving widespread attention at present, three significant legal cases affecting the auditing profession are included in Chapter 4. For these cases, excerpts from the decisions issued by the court are reproduced. The reprint of the cases is preceded by a brief discussion of recent developments concerning the auditor's legal responsibilities.

Chapter 1

The Auditor's Report

The auditor's report is the culmination of the audit. It is the most critical part of the audit process for it is the visible representation on which outsiders will rely. Thus, the report must convey clearly the scope of the work done and the responsibility assumed by the auditor regarding the fairness of financial statements.

Each audit involves gathering adequate evidence about the client's financial statements through whatever means the auditor deems appropriate or necessary. Once the evidence has been assembled, the auditor must sift and weigh that evidence with professional care. He must bring to bear his professional judgment and experience to draw the appropriate conclusions from the evidence he has accumulated. This complex decision-making process carries a very high degree of responsibility. The auditor's decision, which results in his rendering an opinion, is relied upon by third party users who may hold him legally accountable for his opinion.

The Evolution of the Standard Short-Form Report

The standard short-form audit report consists of two basic parts. The *scope* paragraph, which is usually the opening paragraph, gives the reader a summary description of the audit work performed. The *opinion* paragraph contains the auditor's conclusions concerning the financial statements.

The wording of the standard short-form report in general use today was adopted by the accounting profession in 1948. Minor variations in wordings are used but most auditors use the standard wording recommended in Statement No. 33 as follows:

> We have examined the balance sheet of X Company as of June 30, 19— and the related statement(s) of income and retained earnings for the year then ended. Our examination was made in accordance with generally accepted auditing standards, and accordingly included

such tests of the accounting records and such other auditing procedures as we considered necessary in the circumstances.

In our opinion, the accompanying balance sheet and statement(s) of income and retained earnings present fairly the financial position of X Company at June 30, 19—, and the results of its operations for the year then ended, in conformity with generally accepted accounting principles applied on a basis consistent with that of the preceding year.

The audit report has undergone various changes over the years. American auditing practices and procedures during the late 1800's and early 1900's were heavily influenced by British practices. Typical wording of the audit report around 1900 was as follows:

We have audited the books and accounts of the ABC company for the year ended December 31, 19—, and we certify that, in our opinion, the above balance sheet correctly sets forth its position as at the termination of that year and that the accompanying profit and loss account is correct.

It is interesting to note that the above wording referred to an audit of the "books and accounts" rather than the financial statements and that the auditor "certified" the statements as being "correct" or "correctly set forth."

The growth in use of audit reports and the advances in the profession paved the way for a more careful and precise wording of the audit report. In addition, the *Ultramares* decision of 1931, a landmark case extending the auditor's legal responsibility to third party users for gross negligence or constructive fraud, caused a major change in the wording of the audit report. The *Journal of Accountancy* of July 1931, in commenting editorially on the consequences of the *Ultramares* decision, said,

The word "certify" which has been used for many years is quite inappropriate and should be abandoned.

The profession had come to recognize clearly that it was unwise to continue to use the word "certify" or similar words in the audit opinion. The word "certify" conveyed the notion that the contents of the financial statements are subject to precise measurements and that the auditor was capable of guaranteeing the exactness of the data in the financial statements. Both connotations of the word are inappropriate for use by the auditor.

Not only was there a movement away from the use of the word "certify," but other events were set in motion to improve further the wording of the audit report. During 1932 a Special Committee of the Institute met with the Committee on Stock List of the New York Stock Exchange. As a result of these meetings, the Institute's Special Committee, in December 1933, recommended the following wording for the audit report:

We have made an examination of the balance sheet of the XYZ Company as at December 31, 1933, and of the statement of income and surplus for the year 1933. In connection therewith we examined or tested accounting records of the Company and other supporting evidence and obtained information and explanations from officers and employees of the Company; we also made a general review of the accounting methods and of the operating and income accounts for the year, but we did not make a detailed audit of the transactions.

In our opinion, based upon such examination, the accompanying balance sheet and related statement of income and surplus fairly present, in accordance with accepted principles of accounting consistently maintained by the Company during the year under review, its position at December 31, 1933, and the results of its operations for the year.

The wording of the audit report recommended in 1933 clearly avoids the use of the word "certify" and introduces the concepts of fair presentation and consistency of application of accepted accounting principles. The opening paragraph in the Special Committee report reveals an attempt to expand and clarify the scope of the examination.

In 1939 the Institute issued Statement No. 1 entitled "Extensions of Auditing Procedures." This statement was prompted by disclosures of major fraud in *McKesson & Robbins, Inc.*, involving fictitious inventory items and accounts receivable which the audited financial statements failed to reveal. Accordingly, "Extensions of Auditing Procedures" called for revision in the examination of inventories and receivables and suggested a change in the form of the audit report. The statement recommended that the scope paragraph contain a specific reference to a review of the internal control system and that the reference to obtaining information from officers and employees be eliminated. Further, the opinion paragraph was changed to refer to the application of generally accepted accounting principles "on a basis consistent with that of the preceding year" and the financial statements were said to "present fairly" instead of "fairly present" financial position and results of operations. Following the extensive and highly publicized investigations by the Securities and Exchange Commission into the *McKesson & Robbins* case, the Commission in 1941 directed that the auditor must state whether his examination was made in accordance with "generally accepted auditing standards" and whether all procedures considered necessary had been carried out.

The Institute promptly recommended a change in the wording of the audit report to comply with the SEC's requirements. The wording of the audit report recommended in 1941 appears below:

We have examined the balance sheet of the XYZ Company as of February 28, 1941, and the statements of income and surplus for the fiscal year then ended, have reviewed the system of internal control and the accounting procedures of the company and, without making a detailed audit of the transactions, have examined or tested accounting records of the company and other supporting evidence, by methods and to the extent we deemed appropriate. Our examination was made in accordance with generally accepted auditing standards applicable in the circumstances and included all procedures which we considered necessary.

In our opinion, the accompanying balance sheet and related statements of income and surplus present fairly the position of the XYZ Company at February 28, 1941, and the results of its operations for the fiscal year, in conformity with generally accepted accounting principles applied on a basis consistent with that of the preceding year.

In 1944 changes were made again in the scope paragraph by dropping the reference to some of the specific procedures carried out by the auditor. These changes were based on the recognition that the phrase "generally accepted auditing standards" made the enumeration of audit procedures redundant. It was felt that the reader of the report should and would rely on the professional judgment of the auditor to carry out whatever procedures are necessary to satisfy the auditing standards.

In 1948 the audit report was finally changed to the basic form which is in use today. Continuing changes and improvements are taking place in auditing and these are likely to be reflected in the wording of the audit report in the future.

Supplementary wording or phrases, such as reference in the scope paragraph to the examination of the prior year's financial statements and the inclusion of the funds statement in the scope and opinion paragraphs, are frequently used and are illustrated herein.[1]

The Standard Short-Form Report

The auditor's report is a form of technical communication, i.e., the format of the report is structured and the message is couched in specialized and restricted terminology. Various features of the content and meaning of the audit report are discussed below.

Addressee of Auditor's Report

The audit report should be addressed to the client company or to its board of directors. Whenever the auditor's appointment has been formally approved by the stockholders, the report should be addressed to both the stockholders and the board of directors.

---

[1] In March 1971, the Accounting Principles Board of the AICPA issued APB Opinion No. 19 "Reporting Changes in Financial Position." In this opinion the Accounting Principles Board concluded that "When financial statements purporting to present both financial position (balance sheet) and results of operations (statement of income and retained earnings) are issued, a statement summarizing changes in financial position should also be presented as a basic financial statement for each period for which an income statement is presented." The Board also recommended that the title be "Statement of Changes in Financial Position."

The timing of the issuance of this opinion was such that it was not feasible to incorporate herein the changes which the Board made in the traditional funds statement. The reader should study this opinion carefully and consider its effect on illustrations and cases in this book.

Dating of Auditor's Report

Statement No. 33 suggests that the date of the audit report coincide with the date of completion of all important audit procedures by the auditor. If the dating of the audit report is delayed beyond this completion date, this fact should be clearly stated in the report unless the auditor elects to continue inquiries (but not an examination) up to the later date, in which case no special comment is necessary.

Signing of Auditor's Report

The audit report is customarily signed in the name of the auditing firm. The individual member of the firm directing the audit does not use his own signature unless specifically requested. Responsibility for the report rests with the auditing firm. If a firm has offices in several cities, the report should show the location of the office issuing the report.

Scope of Audit

The auditor uses his professional judgment to determine the nature and extent of evidence which he must gather in the performance of an examination. Thus, the audit procedures which the auditor uses and the method and extent of their application will vary from one client to another or from year to year. However, in *all* instances, the auditing procedures carried out must measure up to the profession's generally accepted auditing standards.

Generally Accepted Auditing Standards

The generally accepted auditing standards referred to in the scope paragraph have been approved and adopted by the members of the Institute. They are as follows:

General Standards

1. The examination is to be performed by a person or persons having adequate technical training and proficiency as an auditor.
2. In all matters relating to the assignment, an independence in mental attitude is to be maintained by the auditor or auditors.
3. Due professional care is to be exercised in the performance of the examination and the preparation of the report.

Standards of Field Work

1. The work is to be adequately planned and assistants, if any, are to be properly supervised.

2. There is to be a proper study and evaluation of the existing internal control as a basis for reliance thereon and for the determination of the resultant extent of the tests to which auditing procedures are to be restricted.
3. Sufficient competent evidential matter is to be obtained through inspection, observation, inquiries and confirmations to afford a reasonable basis for an opinion regarding the financial statements under examination.

Standards of Reporting

1. The report shall state whether the financial statements are presented in accordance with generally accepted principles of accounting.
2. The report shall state whether such principles have been consistently observed in the current period in relation to the preceding period.
3. Informative disclosures in the financial statements are to be regarded as reasonably adequate unless otherwise stated in the report.
4. The report shall contain either an expression of opinion regarding the financial statements, taken as a whole, or an assertion to the effect that an opinion cannot be expressed. When an overall opinion cannot be expressed, the reasons therefor should be stated. In all cases where an auditor's name is associated with financial statements, the report should contain a clear-cut indication of the character of the auditor's examination, if any, and the degree of responsibility he is taking.

The Opinion Paragraph

The opinion is, above all, an informed judgment or belief of a professional auditor, a person with adequate technical training and proficiency as an auditor. A clear expression of opinion is called for by the standards of reporting. Furthermore, the auditor must indicate the nature of his examination and the degree of responsibility he assumes.

In formulating his opinion, the auditor must make unequivocal statements regarding several aspects of the client's financial statements. The auditor must state whether the financial statements are presented fairly in conformity with generally accepted accounting principles and whether such principles have been applied consistently. Also, the auditor must see that the financial statements contain sufficient information to make them informative and reliable to the users. In all cases, the auditor must express an opinion on the client's financial statements taken as a whole, or, if appropriate, state clearly that an opinion cannot be expressed and the reasons for the disclaimer.

Illustrations of the Auditor's Report [2]

This section contains a series of illustrations of audit reports. These model reports provide a guide to the reader in developing solutions to the various cases in the book. The wording of the illustrations is based on Statement No. 33 and subsequent statements. These statements constitute an authoritative guide for the auditor, and material departures should be undertaken only with great care.

Illustrations 1 through 4 show various forms of the unqualified audit report. Departures from the unqualified report are covered in Illustrations 5 through 8. Illustrations 9 through 12 relate to various circumstances which require a departure from the standard short-form report. Illustration 13 contains a model of the long-form report.

Where appropriate, the model reports refer to the statement of stockholders' equity rather than to the statement of retained earnings referred to in model wording on page 3. This reference is consistent with the requirement of APB Opinion No. 12 which calls for disclosure of current changes in the separate accounts comprising stockholders' equity when both financial position and results of operations are presented in financial statements.

---

[2]See footnote on page 6.

Standard Short-Form Report
(Statement No. 33: Chapter 10, Paragraph 6)

February 15, 1971

To the Stockholders and Board of Directors,
 XYZ Corporation:

We have examined the balance sheet of XYZ Corporation as of December 31, 1970, and the related statements of income and stockholders' equity for the year then ended. Our examination was made in accordance with generally accepted auditing standards, and accordingly included such tests of the accounting records and such other auditing procedures as we considered necessary in the circumstances.

In our opinion, the accompanying balance sheet and statements of income and stockholders' equity present fairly the financial position of XYZ Corporation as of December 31, 1970, and the results of its operations for the year then ended, in conformity with generally accepted accounting principles applied on a basis consistent with that of the preceding year.

Standard Short-Form Report
Covering Comparative Statements
(Statement No. 33: Chapter 10, Paragraph 48)

February 15, 1971

To the Stockholders and Board of Directors,
  XYZ Corporation:

We have examined the balance sheet of XYZ Corporation as of December 31, 1970, and the related statements of income and stockholders' equity for the year then ended. Our examination was made in accordance with generally accepted auditing standards, and accordingly included such tests of the accounting records and such other auditing procedures as we considered necessary in the circumstances. We previously examined and reported on the financial statements for the preceding year.

In our opinion, the accompanying balance sheet and statements of income and stockholders' equity present fairly the financial position of XYZ Corporation as of December 31, 1970, and the results of its operations for the year then ended, in conformity with generally accepted accounting principles applied on a basis consistent with that of the preceding year.

Note: The only departure from the standard short-form report (Illustration No. 1) is the addition of the last sentence of the first paragraph. An alternative approach would be to extend the opinion to cover the prior year; if this were done, the consistency reference would read ". . . applied on a consistent basis." (Statement No. 33: Chapter 8, Paragraph 14.)

ILLUSTRATION NO. 3

Standard Short-Form Report
Covering Supplemental Schedules

February 15, 1971

To the Stockholders and Board of Directors,
  XYZ Corporation:

We have examined the balance sheet of **XYZ** Corporation as of December 31, 1970, and the related statements of income and stockholders' equity and the supplemental schedules of property and equipment and accumulated depreciation for the year then ended. Our examination was made in accordance with generally accepted auditing standards, and accordingly included such tests of the accounting records and such other auditing procedures as we considered necessary in the circumstances.

In our opinion, the accompanying balance sheet and statements of income and stockholders' equity present fairly the financial position of XYZ Corporation as of December 31, 1970, and the results of its operations for the year then ended, in conformity with generally accepted accounting principles applied on a basis consistent with that of the preceding year; and the supplemental schedules present fairly the information shown therein.

Standard Short-Form Report
with Funds Statement
(APB Opinion No. 3)[3]

February 15, 1971

To the Stockholders and Board of Directors,
XYZ Corporation:

We have examined the balance sheet of XYZ Corporation as of December 31, 1970, and the related statements of income and stockholders' equity and source and application of funds for the year then ended. Our examination was made in accordance with generally accepted auditing standards, and accordingly included such tests of the accounting records and such other auditing procedures as we considered necessary in the circumstances.

In our opinion, the accompanying balance sheet and statements of income and stockholders' equity and source and application of funds present fairly the financial position of XYZ Corporation as of December 31, 1970, and the results of its operations and the source and application of its funds for the year then ended, in conformity with generally accepted accounting principles applied on a basis consistent with that of the preceding year.

[3]Superseded by Opinion No. 19. See footnote on page 6.

Qualified Opinion
(Statement No. 33: Chapter 10, Paragraph 9)

February 15, 1971

To the Stockholders and Board of Directors,
   XYZ Corporation:

We have examined the balance sheet of XYZ Corporation as of December 31, 1970, and the related statements of income and stockholders' equity for the year then ended. Our examination was made in accordance with generally accepted auditing standards, and accordingly included such tests of the accounting records and such other auditing procedures as we considered necessary in the circumstances.

In our opinion, subject to the ultimate effect of the income tax litigation referred to in Note 2 to the financial statements, the accompanying balance sheet and statements of income and stockholders' equity present fairly the financial position of XYZ Corporation as of December 31, 1970, and the results of its operations for the year then ended, in conformity with generally accepted accounting principles applied on a basis consistent with that of the preceding year.

Note: The phrase "subject to" is appropriate for this qualified opinion because the outcome of a matter is uncertain. In other circumstances, the qualifying phrase would be either "except for" or "with the exception."

Adverse Opinion
(Statement No. 33: Chapter 10, Paragraphs 12, 13, and 37)

February 15, 1971

To the Stockholders and Board of Directors,
    XYZ Corporation:

We have examined the balance sheet of XYZ Corporation as of December 31, 1970, and the related statements of income and stockholders' equity for the year then ended. Our examination was made in accordance with generally accepted auditing standards, and accordingly included such tests of the accounting records and such other auditing procedures as we considered necessary in the circumstances.

Although the proceeds of sales are collectible on the installment basis over a five-year period, revenue from such sales is recorded in full by the Company at time of sale. However, for income tax purposes, income is reported only as collections are received and no provision has been made for income taxes on installments to be collected in the future, as required by generally accepted accounting principles. If such provisions had been made, net income for 1970 and retained earnings as of December 31, 1970, would have been reduced by approximately $175,000 and $490,000, respectively, and the balance sheet would have included a liability for deferred income taxes of approximately $490,000.

Because of the materiality of the amounts of omitted income taxes as described in the preceding paragraph, we are of the opinion that the accompanying balance sheet and statements of income and stockholders' equity do not present fairly the financial position of XYZ Corporation as of December 31, 1970, or the results of its operations for the year then ended in conformity with generally accepted accounting principles.

Disclaimer of Opinion
(Statement No. 33: Chapter 10, Paragraphs 14, 15, 16, and 31)

February 15, 1971

To the Stockholders and Board of Directors,
  XYZ Corporation:

We have examined the balance sheet of XYZ Corporation as of December 31, 1970, and the related statements of income and stockholders' equity for the year then ended. Our examination was made in accordance with generally accepted auditing standards, and accordingly included such tests of the accounting records and such other auditing procedures as we considered necessary in the circumstances, except that, in accordance with your instructions, we did not observe the physical inventory taken on December 31, 1970, nor did we request confirmation of balances as of December 31, 1970, directly with the Company's customers and creditors.

Because the assets and liabilities to which the omitted auditing procedures relate enter materially into the determination of financial position and results of operations, we do not express an opinion on the accompanying financial statements taken as a whole.

Piecemeal Opinion
(Statement No. 46)

February 15, 1971

To the Stockholders and Board of Directors,
XYZ Corporation:

We have examined the balance sheet of XYZ Corporation as of December 31, 1970, and the related statements of income and stockholders' equity for the year then ended. Our examination was made in accordance with generally accepted auditing standards, and accordingly included such tests of the accounting records and such other auditing procedures as we considered necessary in the circumstances.

The Company's principal asset consists of its investment in a shopping center which commenced operation in March 1969, and which has operated at a loss through December 31, 1970. Recovery of the investment is dependent upon the success of future operations.

Because of the materiality of the above-mentioned investment, the recovery of which is uncertain, we do not express any opinion on the accompanying financial statements of XYZ Corporation as of December 31, 1970, or for the year then ended, taken as a whole. In our opinion, however, the amounts shown in the accompanying financial statements for current assets, current liabilities, long-term debt, and income and expenses (exclusive of depreciation) are fairly presented in conformity with generally accepted accounting principles applied on a basis consistent with that of the preceding year.

Scope Limitation
(Statement No. 33: Chapter 10, Paragraphs 27 through 29)

February 15, 1971

To the Stockholders and Board of Directors,
   XYZ Corporation:

We have examined the balance sheet of XYZ Corporation as of December 31, 1970, and the related statements of income and stockholders' equity for the year then ended. Our examination was made in accordance with generally accepted auditing standards, and accordingly included such tests of the accounting records and such other auditing procedures as we considered necessary in the circumstances, except that, because of the inadequacy of prior-year records, we were unable to obtain sufficient evidence to form an opinion as to the basis on which the property and related accumulated depreciation are stated.

In our opinion, except for the effect of any adjustments which might be required with respect to the property and related accumulated depreciation accounts, the accompanying balance sheet and statements of income and stockholders' equity present fairly the financial position of XYZ Corporation as of December 31, 1970, and the results of its operations for the year then ended, in conformity with generally accepted accounting principles applied on a basis consistent with that of the preceding year.

Failure to Present Fairly
(Statement No. 33: Chapter 10, Paragraph 37)

February 15, 1971

To the Stockholders and Board of Directors,
    XYZ Corporation:

We have examined the balance sheet of XYZ Corporation as of December 31, 1970, and the related statements of income and stockholders' equity for the year then ended. Our examination was made in accordance with generally accepted auditing standards, and accordingly included such tests of the accounting records and such other auditing procedures as we considered necessary in the circumstances.

In pricing its inventories, the company included only material and direct labor costs. If manufacturing overhead costs had been included in accordance with generally accepted accounting principles, the inventory amount shown in the accompanying balance sheet would have been increased by approximately $492,000 at December 31, 1970, and net income for the year then ended would have been increased by approximately $196,000.

In our opinion, except for the effect of excluding manufacturing overhead costs in the pricing of inventories, the accompanying balance sheet and statements of income and stockholders' equity present fairly the financial position of XYZ Corporation as of December 31, 1970, and the results of its operations for the year then ended, in conformity with generally accepted accounting principles applied on a basis consistent with that of the preceding year.

Lack of Consistency
(Statement No. 33: Chapter 8, Paragraph 18)

February 15, 1971

To the Stockholders and Board of Directors,
   XYZ Corporation:

We have examined the balance sheet of XYZ Corporation as of December 31, 1970, and the related statements of income and stockholders' equity for the year then ended. Our examination was made in accordance with generally accepted auditing standards, and accordingly included such tests of the accounting records and such other auditing procedures as we considered necessary in the circumstances.

As explained in Note 1 to the financial statements, effective January 1, 1970, the company changed from an accelerated to the straight-line method of providing for depreciation of its plant and equipment.

In our opinion, the accompanying balance sheet and statements of income and stockholders' equity present fairly the financial position of XYZ Corporation as of December 31, 1970, and the results of its operations for the year then ended, in conformity with generally accepted accounting principles applied on a basis consistent with that of the preceding year, except for the change to an accepted alternative method of providing for depreciation as noted above.

Uncertainties
(Statement No. 33: Chapter 10, Paragraphs 45 through 47)

February 15, 1971

To the Stockholders and Board of Directors,
  XYZ Corporation:

    We have examined the balance sheet of XYZ Corporation as of December 31, 1970, and the related statements of income and stockholders' equity for the year then ended. Our examination was made in accordance with generally accepted auditing standards, and accordingly included such tests of the accounting records and such other auditing procedures as we considered necessary in the circumstances.

    The receivables in the accompanying balance sheet include $238,309 due from franchisees of the company's stores. A provision has been made for uncollectible receivables as of December 31, 1970; however, the collection experience with franchisees is limited since these operations have been conducted for only a short time (approximately two years). Accordingly, the ultimate collectibility of these receivables and any losses that may be sustained therefrom are not reasonably determinable at this time.

    In our opinion, subject to the reasonableness of the provision for uncollectible receivables, the accompanying balance sheet and statements of income and stockholders' equity present fairly the financial position of XYZ Corporation as of December 31, 1970, and the results of its operations for the year then ended, in conformity with generally accepted accounting principles applied on a basis consistent with that of the preceding year.

ILLUSTRATION NO. 13

Long-Form Report
(Statement No. 33: Chapter 12)

February 15, 1971

To the Stockholders and Board of Directors,
    XYZ Corporation:

We have examined the balance sheet of XYZ Corporation as of December 31, 1970, and the related statements of income and stockholders' equity for the year then ended. Our examination was made in accordance with generally accepted auditing standards, and accordingly included such tests of the accounting records and such other auditing procedures as we considered necessary in the circumstances. Our more significant auditing procedures are set forth on page 10 of this report. We previously examined and reported on the financial statements for the preceding year.

In our opinion, the accompanying balance sheet and statements of income and stockholders' equity present fairly the financial position of XYZ Corporation as of December 31, 1970, and the results of its operations for the year then ended, in conformity with generally accepted accounting principles applied on a basis consistent with that of the preceding year.

Our examination has been made primarily for the purpose of formulating the opinion set forth in the preceding paragraph. The data included in pages 2 to 9 and schedules I to IV of this report, although not considered necessary for a fair presentation of the financial position and results of operations, are presented for supplementary analysis purposes and have been subjected to the audit procedures applied in the examination of the basic financial statements. In our opinion, these data are fairly stated in all material respects in relation to the basic financial statements, taken as a whole.

Financial and Operating Highlights

(This section would contain a summary of the more significant balance sheet and income statement items and would include significant ratios.)

Comments on Financial Position

(In this section, the auditor would comment on the reasons for changes in financial position at the end of the current year as compared to the end of the preceding year. Various analyses might be included as a basis for these comments.)

Comments on Results of Operations

(In this section, the auditor would comment on the reasons for increases or decreases in income, expenses, gross profit and net income for the current year as compared to the preceding year. Various tabulations might be included as a basis for these comments.)

Scope of Examination

(This section would contain a description of the scope of the auditors' examination that would be more detailed than the description in the usual short-form report.)

Very truly yours,

Analytical Guide in Preparing the Auditor's Report

In formulating his opinion and writing his report, the auditor should follow a systematic framework of analysis. This section presents a guide to steps the auditor should follow in drafting his report. The reader will find this guide to be a valuable aid in developing solutions to the cases in Chapters 2 and 3.

In making an examination of the financial statements, the auditor must be satisfied that the following conditions exist:

1. His examination is in accordance with generally accepted auditing standards.
2. The financial statements have been prepared in conformity with generally accepted accounting principles.
3. The generally accepted accounting principles have been consistently applied.
4. Adequate disclosure has been made of information essential for a fair presentation.
5. No unusual uncertainties exist concerning future developments.

If one or more of the above conditions are not satisfied, the auditor must determine whether or not the circumstances will require a deviation from the standard short-form report and if it will, the extent of such deviation.

The following logical sequential approach can be followed in most instances in preparing the auditor's report:

1. Determine the circumstances that may require deviation from the standard short-form report. The usual circumstances, as categorized in Chapter 10 of Statement No. 33, are as follows:

   A. The scope of the auditor's examination is limited or affected:
      (1) By conditions which preclude the application of auditing procedures considered necessary in the circumstances.
      (2) By restrictions imposed by clients.
      (3) Because part of the examination has been made by other independent auditors.

   B. The financial statements do not present fairly financial position or results of operations because of:
      (1) Lack of conformity with generally accepted accounting principles.
      (2) Inadequate disclosure.

C. Accounting principles are not consistently applied.

D. Unusual uncertainties exist concerning future developments, the effects of which cannot be reasonably estimated or otherwise resolved satisfactorily.

2. Consider materiality, both with respect to financial position and to results of operations. Although materiality is one of the greatest judgmental factors facing the auditor, some general guidelines have been developed in this area. Discussions of materiality can be found in Accounting Research Study No. 7 (pages 38 through 41), and in Statement No. 33 (Chapter 10).

3. If the effect of the circumstances outlined above is considered material, evaluate the degree of materiality and determine the appropriate departure from the standard short-form report.

4. If the deviation from the standard short-form report is due to:

A. Scope limitation or uncertainties —
Determine whether a qualified opinion or a disclaimer of opinion should be given.

B. Lack of fairness of presentation —
Determine whether a qualified opinion or an adverse opinion should be given.

C. Inconsistent application of accounting principles —
Determine what comment should be made with respect to consistency.

Qualified opinions, adverse opinions, and disclaimers of opinion are described in Chapter 10 of Statement No. 33 while consistency problems are discussed in Chapter 8.

5. If a qualified opinion is to be given, determine the appropriate qualifying words, either "except for" or "subject to." In general, the words "except for" are recommended in all cases other than those in which the outcome of a matter is uncertain and the effect cannot be reasonably estimated; in these latter cases the words "subject to" are appropriate.

6. If a disclaimer of opinion or an adverse opinion is to be given, consider the appropriateness and nature of a "piecemeal" opinion. A description of a "piecemeal" opinion together with limitations on its use are contained in Statement No. 46.

Chapter 2
Departures From The Standard Short-Form Report

Statement No. 33 classifies circumstances requiring a departure from the standard short-form report into four categories. This chapter contains groupings of cases which illustrate the four types of circumstances requiring a departure from the standard short-form report. Section A deals with cases in which the auditor is faced with limitations in the scope of his examination. In Section B the predominant issue in the cases is that of fairness of presentation. Several cases involving a question of consistency of application of accounting principles are included in Section C. Section D contains cases dealing with the existence of unusual uncertainties in financial statements.

The cases have been grouped for the convenience of the reader and several of the cases may involve more than one of the circumstances requiring a departure from the standard short-form report.

Limitations in Scope of Examination

The audit examination must be thorough in all respects and must not be limited in scope. If the auditor encounters limitations in his audit, these must be carefully assessed and may lead to a qualification or a disclaimer of opinion. Limitations in scope can be broken down into three categories. These are outlined in Statement No. 33 as (1) conditions which preclude the application of auditing procedures considered necessary in the circumstances, (2) restrictions which are imposed by the client, and (3) examination having been made in part by other independent auditors. Cases in this section illustrate circumstances in which limitations in scope are an issue. Other issues also arise in each of the cases.

Hess & Riker, Inc.

Hess & Riker, Inc., is a midwest company engaged in the manufacture and sale of dairy products and candy. Since its beginning, the company has used December 31 as its year-end date. It has been audited by Atwood & Atwood, CPA's, each year, including the year ended December 31, 1969. An unqualified opinion was issued in each instance by the auditors.

In March 1970, Hess & Riker entered into negotiations with Arrowhead Products, Inc., a New York based firm, for the merger of Hess & Riker into Arrowhead. Agreement was reached and the merger was accomplished as of July 1, 1970. Arrowhead, whose fiscal year ends June 30th, requested that Hess & Riker submit a balance sheet as of June 30, 1970, and an income statement for the twelve months then ended. These statements were to be accompanied by an audit opinion prepared by Atwood & Atwood. Financial data in part from the Hess & Riker financial statements appeared as follows:

June 30, 1970

Current Assets (Including inventory of $2,060,000)	$ 6,940,000
Total Assets	10,220,000
Current Liabilities	4,100,000
Stockholders' Equity	5,710,000

12 Months Ended June 30, 1970

Total Revenues	$ 8,380,000
Net Income	1,020,000

Atwood & Atwood had no difficulty in satisfying itself as to the fairness of the financial position of Hess & Riker as of June 30, 1970. However, in reviewing operations for the twelve months ended June 30, 1970, Atwood & Atwood found that while the company maintained a perpetual inventory system, these records were not completely reliable. Hess & Riker had taken a physical count of the inventory on December 31 of each year and had adjusted its inventory records to agree with the physical count. In the past these differences had, on the average, amounted to 10% of the dollar amount of the inventory. Atwood & Atwood had observed the company's inventory count on December 31, 1968 and 1969. The company did not take an inventory on June 30, 1969; the inventory at that date was based on perpetual inventory records.

Issues for consideration:

(1) Should the auditors issue an unqualified opinion on the statements taken as a whole for the year ended June 30, 1970? Explain why or why not. Suggest appropriate wording for the opinion.

(2) The beginning inventory for the year ended June 30, 1970, falls in the middle of a period which was previously attested to by the auditors. What effect, if any, should this have on the auditors' ability to satisfy themselves as to the June 30, 1969, inventory?

National Industries, Inc.

National Industries, Inc., is a large East Coast manufacturer and distributor of plumbing and bathroom fixtures. The company has a number of subsidiaries, most of which are included in National's consolidated financial statements. The financial statements of National and its subsidiaries are audited each year by Allen & Baker, CPA's.

In making its examination for the year ended March 31, 1970, Allen & Baker attempted to obtain evidence in support of a miscellaneous investment account in the amount of $1,056,000. Most of the investment had been made in January and February of 1970. The company records examined by the auditors contained no information as to the nature of the investment. Financial data in part from the financial statements appeared as follows:

March 31, 1970

Current Assets	$62,348,000
Investments and Advances	4,422,000
Total Assets	99,405,000
Stockholders' Equity	85,883,000

12 Months Ended March 31, 1970

Net Income	$ 3,731,000

In pursuing the question of the unsupported investment with top management, the auditors were informed that National was supplying funds to a New York bank to buy securities for National's account. However, management did not wish to disclose the identity of the investment. All other information regarding the investment was provided to the auditor including a confirmation direct from the bank that acknowledged the receipt of the funds from National and the purchase of securities. In addition, the bank provided information as to the quoted market value of these securities as of March 31, 1970, and the income earned by the company thereon for the year then ended. This income had been recorded in the proper period by the company.

Issues for consideration:

(1) Should the auditors issue an unqualified opinion? Explain.

(2) Should the auditors require a "representation letter" from management on this issue? If so, what should it include?

Lincoln Supply, Inc.

Robertson & Black, a CPA firm, was engaged by Jackson Corp. to audit the financial statements of Lincoln Supply, Inc., a distributor of major appliances, as of October 31, 1970. Jackson Corp. is gathering information on Lincoln Supply, Inc., pursuant to a proposed acquisition of Lincoln Supply.

The firm of Robertson & Black has been the auditors for Jackson Corp. for many years. Prior to 1970 Lincoln Supply was audited by another firm of CPA's.

In performing the examination, Robertson & Black was instructed by the president of Jackson Corp. not to circularize Lincoln's customers which were principally retail stores. The president explained that Lincoln's customers were operating at the peak of their seasonal business and requests for confirmation would place an undue burden on them. In addition, the president stated that Lincoln's records were in good condition and that the auditors should have no difficulty in verifying the receivables.

Below are partial data from Lincoln's financial statements:

October 31, 1970

Receivables (Net of an allowance of $1,350,000)	$24,560,000
Other Current Assets	13,385,000
Total Assets	47,288,000
Stockholders' Equity	28,176,000

12 Months Ended October 31, 1970

Sales	$43,940,000
Net Income	3,271,000

During the examination of Lincoln, Robertson & Black took the following steps in its review of receivables. The accounts receivable balances at October 31 were compared with those of prior periods and differences were explained satisfactorily. The schedules of aged accounts and bad debt charge-offs were reviewed and no unusual items were noted. The month of April was selected as a test period and all general ledger account transactions were analyzed and found to be in agreement with source records. The internal control review did not reveal any serious inadequacies. In addition, Robertson & Black reviewed the working papers of Lincoln's prior auditors and noted that receivables had been circularized in the past with satisfactory results.

Issues for consideration:

(1) Should Robertson & Black issue an unqualified opinion in the above circumstances? Explain.

(2) What additional audit procedures, if any, should have been carried out by the auditor? What effect would these additional procedures have on the auditor's opinion?

Central Electronics, Inc.

The auditing firm of Moreland, Miller & Co. was engaged in May 1970, to conduct an audit of Central Electronics, Inc., for the year ended June 30, 1970. Central is a fast growing manufacturer of radios and electronic components. It is planning to sell stock to the public in the latter part of 1970 and then apply for listing on a national stock exchange. As a result of its planned public offering, Central requested that the auditors issue an opinion on its income statement for the year ended June 30, 1969.

In the past, Central has called upon a small CPA firm, Witlow & Co., for assistance in preparing its tax returns, but Central's financial statements have not been audited prior to May 1970.

Summary financial data for Central are as follows:

	June 30		
	1968	1969	1970
Inventories	$ 477,000	$ 513,000	$ 681,000
Other Current Assets	907,000	1,120,000	1,349,000
Plant and Other Assets (Net) ..	511,000	602,000	730,000
Total Assets	$1,895,000	$2,235,000	$2,760,000
Current Liabilities	$ 980,000	$1,238,000	$1,446,000
Stockholders' Equity	915,000	997,000	1,314,000
Total Equities	$1,895,000	$2,235,000	$2,760,000

	12 Months Ended June 30		
	1968	1969	1970
Sales	$2,163,000	$2,468,000	$2,730,000
Net Income (Before taxes)	447,000	524,000	718,000

Moreland, Miller & Co. carried out all auditing procedures considered necessary to render an opinion as Central requested, except the observing of the inventory taken at June 30, 1968 and 1969. In order to satisfy themselves as to the reliability of the beginning inventories, the auditors took the following steps.

Quantities:

(1) Made cut-off tests of shipments and receipts at the beginning and end of each year.

(2) Tested the accumulation of the physical inventory as of June 30, 1969, by using the original detail count sheets. Detail count sheets were not available for the June 30, 1968, inventory.

(3) The company maintained perpetual records (not related to accounting system) on major items of raw materials. Quantities from the perpetual records were traced to the physical inventory count sheets on a test basis. No significant differences were noted.

(4) Selected items from the June 30, 1970, inventory were "traced back" to June 30, 1969, by using receiving and usage reports and other production department records. All differences disclosed in inventory quantities were satisfactorily explained. A few items were "traced back" to June 30, 1968.

(5) Physical inventory quantities and procedures were discussed thoroughly with operating personnel.

(6) Overall tests, including gross profit percentages and turnovers, were made and variations were satisfactorily explained by management.

Pricing:

(1) Prices in the June 1968 and 1969 inventories were compared with suppliers' invoices and cost estimates.

(2) The amount of overhead in the inventories was tested.

(3) Prices for certain items were compared to net realizable values.

(4) A test was made for obsolescence.

(5) It was determined that the inventory had been priced on a consistent basis.

Clerical:

(1) Clerical accuracy of detail count sheets was verified.
(2) The priced inventories were traced to general ledger balances.

The work performed on the 1968 and 1969 inventories plus the auditors' examination and observation of the 1970 inventory caused the auditors to feel that the accounting records were reliable. In addition, the auditors felt that any error in the inventories would have to be substantial before net income would be materially affected.

Issues for consideration:

(1) What type of opinion should the auditors issue on Central Electronics?
(2) What bearing did the impending registration of the public offering with the Securities and Exchange Commission have on the decision?
(3) Do you agree that the work performed on the 1968 and 1969 inventories was adequate to satisfy the auditors as to the opening inventory balances?

Whitmore Co. and Kory, Inc.

Whitmore Co. is a widely held company whose stock is traded on the New York stock exchange. During 1970 Whitmore acquired an additional 27% interest in Kory, Inc., and as a result owned 58% of Kory on December 31, 1970. Due to extensive and complex reorganizations being made in Kory's capital structure, Kory's financial statements were not consolidated into those of Whitmore on December 31, 1970. The investment in Kory is included among Other Assets by Whitmore (see below) and is carried in the amount of $6,857,000.

The financial position and results of operations of Whitmore are summarized as follows:

December 31, 1970

Current Assets	$41,340,000
Other Assets (Including investment in Kory on equity basis)	11,769,000
Plant and Equipment (Net)	18,663,000
Total Assets	$71,772,000
Current Liabilities	$24,453,000
Long-Term Debt	6,488,000
Stockholders' Equity	40,831,000
Total Equities	$71,772,000

12 Months Ended December 31, 1970

Sales	$102,645,000
Net Income (Before equity in undistributed earnings of Kory)	$ 9,325,000
Equity (58%) in Earnings of Kory	478,000
Net Income	$ 9,803,000

The firm of Aiken & Bakin, CPA's, has been the auditors for Whitmore for the last ten years. Kory, Inc., was audited by L. A. Greene & Co. for the year ended December 31, 1970. In the course of its audit for the year ended December 31, 1970, Aiken & Bakin was furnished with a copy of the Kory financial statements as audited by Greene. The audit report on Kory's statements contained qualifications relating to receivables and possible tax deficiencies. Excerpts from Greene's report are shown below:

> As explained in Note 4, provisions have been made to cover expected losses from uncollectible receivables. While these provisions reflect management's best current judgment, it is not possible to evaluate the provisions for uncollectible receivables prior to the time the receivables are realized.
>
> In our opinion, subject to any adjustments arising from the realization of receivables referred to above, and subject to the final outcome of the pending tax deficiency described in Note 5, the accompanying financial statements present fairly the financial position of Kory, Inc., at December 31, 1970, and the result of its operations for the year then ended, in conformity with generally accepted accounting principles applied on a basis consistent with that of the preceding year.

The receivables on Kory's balance sheet were reported as $8,644,000 with an allowance for uncollectibles of $2,896,000. Greene reported that due to the financial weakness of several of Kory's major debtors (some of whom were shut down because of a prolonged strike), it was necessary to take exception to the valuation of receivables. A telephone conversation with the partner in charge of the engagement for Greene revealed that he felt that the maximum amount of uncollectible accounts would be about 4 to 5 million dollars.

As a result of an Internal Revenue agent's examination of Kory, a tax deficiency was proposed for the years 1968 and 1969 in the amount of 1.8 million dollars. This deficiency represented 20% of Kory's stockholders' equity. Kory's management and its legal counsel were confident that a major portion of the proposed deficiency would be resolved in favor of the company. Kory's attorney stated in a letter that in his opinion the tax deficiency, when resolved, would not exceed $1,000,000. This information was cited in a footnote to the Kory statements and was included as part of the auditors' qualification on the financial statements.

In preparing the audit report on the financial statements of Whitmore, Mr. Randall, partner for Aiken & Bakin, determined that the only items at issue were the reference to the Greene audit of Kory and the disposition of the exceptions cited by Greene in his report.

Issues for consideration:

(1) What type of opinion should be issued on Whitmore? Suggest the appropriate wording of the audit report.

(2) Should the audit report on Whitmore disclose the fact that the auditors for the Kory subsidiary have issued a qualified opinion on the Kory financial statements?

(3) If Kory had been consolidated, what effect would this have on the auditor's report?

Fairness of Presentation of Financial Statements

The auditor must state whether or not the financial statements of the client are fairly presented. Fairness of presentation is central to the auditor's report and must be evaluated in terms of conformity with generally accepted accounting principles. Moreover, fairness requires that there be adequate disclosure of information in the financial statements.

In his evaluation of the financial statements for fairness of presentation, the auditor must consider the issue of materiality. The determination of the materiality or nonmateriality of an item is not subject to simple rules and must always be viewed in terms of the impact of the item on the decisions of an average investor or other users of financial statements.

The determination of fairness of presentation requires the highest degree of professional acumen and judgment on the part of the auditor. The cases in this section highlight a variety of circumstances, including the consideration of materiality, where the auditor must use his professional skill in resolving issues on fairness.

Kingston Clothiers, Inc.

Kingston Clothiers, Inc., is a closely held company whose shares are held by two families. The company was formed in 1945 to hold and exploit an exclusive franchise from a clothing manufacturer to sell at retail a line of men's suits in a large eastern city. In the ensuing years, additional franchises were obtained for other nearby cities as the clothing line became popular nationwide. The franchises are for periods ranging from 30 to 50 years and some contain renewal options.

The financial statements contained the following summary data:

July 31, 1970

Current Assets	$1,183,000
Property and Equipment (Net of depreciation)	337,000
Franchises	431,000
Appraisal Increase on Franchises (Less related income taxes)	2,518,000
Total Assets	$4,469,000
Current Liabilities	$1,882,000
Common Stock	300,000
Retained Earnings (Deficit)	(231,000)
Appraisal Surplus	2,518,000
Total Equities	$4,469,000

12 Months Ended July 31, 1970

Sales	$1,219,000
Net Loss	301,000

During the year ended July 31, 1970, the president, with the approval of the board of directors, insisted that the appraisal increase be recorded to reflect properly the current value of the exclusive franchises held by Kingston. There was ample evidence that the value of the franchises greatly exceeded their cost. In fact, the president had received unsolicited offers from competitors for certain franchises, which substantiated the appraisal. The auditors advised the president against the inclusion of the appraisal on the balance sheet. They were successful in having the increase shown as a separate item on the balance sheet and recorded net of income taxes which would apply in the event the franchises were sold. The appraisal increase was fully explained in a note attached to the financial statements. The note pointed out that the profit and loss statement had not been affected since the appraisal increment was not being amortized.

Issues for consideration:

(1) Assuming the appraisal increase matter was the only issue raised as a result of the auditor's examination, what type of opinion, if any, should the auditor give on:

    a. The financial statements, taken as a whole?

    b. The balance sheet?

    c. The income statement?

Discuss reasons for your position.

(2) Is a piecemeal opinion called for?

(3) Is a consistency qualification called for?

Federal Bancorp, Inc.

The auditing firm of Wilson and Greg was engaged in December of 1970 to audit the financial statements of Federal Bancorp, Inc., for the year ended December 31, 1970. Federal Bancorp is a holding company whose principal assets consist of the majority interest in the voting stock of several banks and finance companies. The financial statements of these subsidiaries of Federal Bancorp are not consolidated with its financial statements and the audit engagement did not cover the audit of the subsidiaries. However, unaudited financial statements of each of the subsidiaries were furnished to the auditors. These statements were reviewed carefully and, in addition, the auditors visited each of the subsidiary companies. The auditors met with a representative of top management at each of the subsidiaries and discussed the accounting policies followed in the preparation of financial statements. At several banks and at most of the finance companies, the auditors' interview with management was followed by a limited review of the internal control system and its effectiveness. The auditors found no basis on which to question the reasonableness of the subsidiaries' financial statements. A summary of the financial statements of Federal Bancorp appears at the top of the next page.

After considerable discussion within the firm, Wilson and Greg decided to issue an unqualified opinion on Federal Bancorp's financial statements. The auditors insisted that the financial statements be labeled "Parent Company Only."

Issues for consideration:

(1) Discuss the appropriateness of the Wilson and Greg opinion. If the opinion issued was not appropriate, what type of opinion should have been issued? Explain.

(2) Do the financial statements as presented with the attached note constitute a fair presentation of financial position and results of operations? Is the presentation in conformity with generally accepted accounting principles?

(3) How should the investment in the banks and finance companies be valued on the balance sheet? Why?

Balance Sheet
December 31, 1970

Cash and Marketable Securities	$ 689,000
Investments:	
Subsidiary Companies, at cost (Note 3)	
Banks..........................	1,333,000
Finance Companies	890,000
Other Investments	250,000
Other Assets	923,000
Total Assets	$4,085,000
Liabilities	$ 470,000
Capital Stock	3,100,000
Retained Surplus	515,000
Total Equities.......................	$4,085,000

Statement of Operations
For 12 Months Ended December 31, 1970

Income	$ 344,000
Expenses	113,000
Net Income	$ 231,000

Note 3 to the financial statements is reproduced below:

Investments in Banks and Finance Companies

At December 31, 1970, Federal Bancorp's interest in the underlying equity of the banks exceeded the carrying value on the books of Bancorp by approximately $2,500,000. The interest in the underlying equity of the finance companies exceeded the carrying value of Bancorp by approximately $3,200,000.

Dividends received by Bancorp during 1970 amounted to $302,000; the combined net income of the banks and finance companies, after deducting minority interests, was $965,000.

Fulton-Ward, Inc.

Fulton-Ward, Inc., is a chain engaged in the sale, through retail outlets, of better quality women's apparel and accessories. The firm was organized in Chicago in 1945 and has grown rapidly. It now consists of 78 retail outlets throughout the midwest in addition to the central warehousing and administration facilities in Chicago.

During the year ended July 31, 1970, Fulton-Ward opened a large merchandise distribution and data processing center adjacent to its administrative offices in Chicago. The new facility was designed to modernize merchandise handling for the firm and to provide more effective and current information for each of the stores through the use of a large-scale computer complex.

The facility was completed in December 1969 but was not fully staffed until March of 1970. The gross operating costs of the new center amounted to $2,560,000 for the fiscal year. Each store is to be billed for a service charge which will consist of a fixed amount plus a percentage of the cost of the merchandise shipped to each store from the central distribution center. It is expected that when fully operative, the center will run at a near break-even level. Service charges during fiscal 1970 amounted to $802,000; however, the volume handled had not yet reached expected levels.

In preparing financial statements for 1970, the company proposed to defer the costs of the center in excess of the charges made to the stores, an aggregate of $1,758,000. Management considered this to be fully justified because these costs amounted to preoperating and training costs. In fact, the first year's activities were largely in the nature of research and development. According to management the current year's efforts were going to benefit future operations of the company, and management proposed that these deferred charges be amortized over a 5 to 8 year period.

A portion of the significant items on the financial statements, before audit adjustments, appears at the top of the next page.

The auditors were reluctant to endorse cost deferment of the distribution and data processing center in spite of management's insistence.

July 31, 1970

Current Assets	$28,308,000
Fixed Assets	45,755,000
Other Assets (Including deferred charges) . . .	3,178,000
Stockholders' Equity (Including retained earnings of $24,239,000)	49,287,000

12 Months Ended July 31, 1970

Sales for the Year	$83,841,000
Net Income	2,939,000

After careful analysis of the center's activities during the year, the auditors proposed that the costs related to this period, $740,000, be expensed in fiscal 1970. In addition, after reviewing payroll costs and carefully inquiring about training activities prior to the use of the center, the auditors felt that start-up and training costs of $600,000 should be deferred. Furthermore, the auditors recommended that the deferred costs, after appropriate reduction for taxes, be amortized over a five year period.

Issues for consideration:

(1) If management refuses to accept the auditors' recommendations, what type of report should the auditors issue?

(2) Is materiality a critical issue in this case? Note that the net operating costs of $1,758,000 are deductible for income tax purposes whether or not deferred on the balance sheet.

(3) If management agrees with the recommendations of the auditors, (a) how should the deferred costs and the amounts charged against income be shown on the financial statements and (b) what footnote should be appended to the statements to explain the treatment of these costs?

Maradex, Inc.

The independent auditors of Maradex, Inc., have been making an annual examination of the consolidated financial statements of Maradex for several years. In discussing the audit for the year ended March 31, 1970, with the audit partner in charge, the president of Maradex indicated that the scope of the examination should not be limited in any manner, but the opinion should cover the consolidated balance sheet only and should omit any reference to the income statement. He explained that the balance sheet would be used primarily to maintain credit relationships with bankers and suppliers.

A summary of the significant financial statement items appears below:

March 31, 1970

Current Assets	$ 4,345,000
Current Liabilities (Including trade accounts payable and bank loans of $1,886,000) ...	2,773,000
Long-Term Debt	1,639,000
Stockholders' Equity	3,122,000

12 Months Ended March 31, 1970

Net Sales	$10,102,000
Net Loss	153,000

Maradex produces and sells two groups of product lines on a national basis. These groups have had a consistent pattern of profitable operations. Two years ago the management of the company decided to embark upon an expansion program by introducing a third major product line. Extensive costs have been incurred in design, start-up production, market research, and promotion of the new line. As a result of charging these costs against income as incurred, the overall operations of the company showed a loss in 1970. Management is firm in its contention that the new line will operate at break-even in 1971 and that it will contribute substantially to company profits in the future.

Due to Maradex's long history of sound and profitable operations and the optimistic expectations about the future, the president explained to the auditors that the company did not wish to disclose the loss for the year 1970. The president felt that the auditor's report should refer only to the balance sheet and that the analysis of retained earnings should not reveal the amount of the operating loss.

Issues for consideration:

(1) With due consideration to the trend of the company's operations and future expectations, should the auditor issue an opinion on the balance sheet only?

(2) Is it appropriate for the auditor to issue an opinion on the balance sheet only when he is aware that the firm has operated at a loss?

(3) In the circumstances described above, should the auditor question the immediate charge-off of design, start-up, and promotion costs? If the new product line is expected to be profitable in future years, does the balance sheet, which fails to show development costs, present fairly the financial position of the firm? Discuss.

Weber-Ramac Co., Inc.

Weber-Ramac Co., Inc., is a Los Angeles based company which, along with several subsidiaries, is engaged in the manufacture of drugs, dyes, and photographic supplies. One of Weber-Ramac's major subsidiaries was acquired in 1968 at a cost substantially less than its equity in the net assets shown by the subsidiary's books at the date of acquisition.

In 1969 Weber-Ramac, in anticipation of listing its shares on the American Stock Exchange, engaged the public accounting firm of Young Ross, Peter & Bro., CPA's, to conduct an audit of its financial statements for the year ended January 31, 1970.

In preliminary discussions with Weber-Ramac, Allen Pope, the audit partner with Young Ross, learned that Weber-Ramac has always included negative goodwill (the excess of the subsidiary's net book value at date of acquisition over the cost of the investment in the subsidiary) as part of the stockholders' equity in the consolidated statements. As a result, Pope addressed a letter to the president of Weber-Ramac explaining that his firm would probably take exception in its audit report to the treatment of negative goodwill. The president expressed displeasure at the decision reached by Pope but decided to leave the issue pending.

A summary of financial data from the consolidated statements appears below and at the top of the next page.

January 31, 1970

Current Assets	$ 6,866,000
Plant and Equipment (Net)	3,251,000
Total Assets	10,944,000
Current Liabilities	6,162,000
Mortgages Payable	1,204,000
Stockholders' Equity	3,578,000

The auditor's examination revealed that the negative goodwill at January 31, 1970, amounted to $973,000. This item was shown

12 Months Ended January 31, 1970

Sales $12,417,000
Cost of Sales, Selling, and
  General and Administrative Expenses 11,642,000
Net Income 283,000

as part of the stockholders' equity section under "Capital in Excess of Par Value." Pope proposed that the negative goodwill be reported as a separate caption below the liabilities but clearly distinguished from the stockholders' equity section. Pope said that he felt that the negative goodwill constituted a deferred credit or a general valuation reserve since the subsidiary was still operating at a loss ($161,000 for the year ended January 31, 1970). Nevertheless, the president of Weber-Ramac considered the subsidiary as an excellent acquisition with great potential in the future. Thus, he disagreed with the auditor's proposal for a change in the method of reporting negative goodwill on Weber-Ramac's consolidated statements.

Issues for consideration:

(1) What type of opinion should the auditing firm issue on Weber-Ramac's consolidated statements as of January 31, 1970? Give reasons.

(2) What wording would you suggest for a middle paragraph, if any, and for the opinion paragraph?

(3) Comment on the proper treatment of negative goodwill according to generally accepted accounting principles.

(4) Does the reporting issue raised in the above case affect Weber-Ramac's consolidated income statement? Explain.

Ohio Industries, Inc.

Ohio Industries, Inc., is a manufacturer of toys, seat belts, and sports equipment with several plants in Ohio and Indiana.

At January 31, 1970, the audit date, Ohio Industries was considering the sale and leaseback of an undivided half interest in its manufacturing plant and equipment. A summary of Ohio Industries' assets on January 31, 1970, was as follows:

Current Assets	$3,353,000
Investments	981,000
Plant and Equipment (Net)	2,644,000
Other Assets	519,000
Total Assets	$7,497,000

Negotiations in January 1970 called for the sale of an undivided half interest in plant and equipment with a book value of $2,340,000. The properties would then be leased back to Ohio Industries which would have substantially all rights of ownership during the life of the noncancelable lease. The sale, if completed, will greatly improve Ohio Industries' net working capital which was $110,000 at January 31, 1970. The gain on the proposed sale, estimated at about $300,000, is to be deferred and taken into income on the installment method.

A note was appended to the financial statements describing the proposed sale and leaseback of the undivided half interest. The note explained that the buyer, a partnership of several of Ohio's major customers, proposed to "lease back to the company the portion of the plant and equipment purchased, for annual rentals equal to one half of the net profit from plant operations, before depreciation and income taxes." The proposed lease will run for 24 years, after which Ohio can obtain full title to the properties for $50,000.

The effective date of the proposed sale had not been determined at the date of the auditors' report, March 29, 1970, but the management of Ohio Industries indicated that the sale might be made effective as of January 31, 1970.

Issues for consideration:

(1) Should the auditors qualify their opinion on Ohio Industries' financial statements because of the proposed sale and leaseback of the plant and equipment? Explain why or why not.

(2) If the proposed effective date of the sale had been set by the parties as April 1, 1970, what effect would this have had on your position in (1) above?

(3) Discuss the appropriate accounting treatment of a sale-and-leaseback transaction as described in the above case.

(4) What should the auditors' position be if the company refuses to disclose the proposed sale in its financial statements?

Kormel, Inc.

Kormel, Inc., is a publicly owned company listed on a major stock exchange. Pertinent financial data are summarized as follows:

June 30, 1970

Cash	$ 30,000
Trade Receivables	2,456,000
Other Receivables	540,000
Inventories	2,968,000
Other Current Assets	75,000
Total Current Assets	$ 6,069,000
Current Liabilities	5,876,000
Net Current Assets	$ 193,000
Property and Equipment (Net of depreciation)	3,760,000
Long-Term Investments	220,000
Long-Term Debt	(3,410,000)
Net Assets	$ 763,000

12 Months Ended June 30, 1970

Net Sales	$ 14,320,000
Net Loss	827,000

Organization and Operating Results

The company is organized into four manufacturing divisions:

Bremer — luggage and hand bags

Kormer — small equipment for restaurants and cafeterias

Rackson — fasteners and clips

Homco — home appliances

The company was founded in 1949 and experienced a satisfactory level of profit until it began to operate at a loss in the late 1960's. Operations during the last three years have resulted in losses as follows:

Year Ended June 30	Loss before Taxes (000 Omitted)
1970	$ 827
1969	1,610
1968	2,380

Bremer Division Problems

The Bremer Division, the largest of the four divisions, showed a loss of approximately $1,000,000 in 1970 and an examination revealed that this rate of loss would continue during 1971. Sales declined from $16,200,000 in 1968 to $6,100,000 in 1970. At June 30, 1970, receivables of the Bremer Division amounted to $760,000 (net of an allowance of $65,000). Collections on these receivables, while slow, have been steady. However, the company has been forced to relax its credit standards and sell to marginal customers to combat the decline in sales.

The inventories of the Bremer Division at June 30, 1970, are $1,246,000 and are valued at the lower of cost or market. Bremer uses a standard cost system to set the cost of inventories; this cost is below current selling prices. However, if this Division is discontinued and the entire inventory has to be sold in a short period of time, substantial losses would probably be incurred.

Faced with declining sales in the Bremer Division, management has considered the consequences of discontinuing the Bremer Division and liquidating the related receivables and inventories. A careful investigation by the company has indicated that the disposition of the Bremer Division would result in estimated losses of between $400,000 and $700,000. The estimate of potential loss was reviewed by the independent auditors of Kormel who found the estimates to be reasonable. The other divisions of Kormel are operating at a profit. Management feels that these remaining divisions could be expanded to absorb any slack caused by the disposition of Bremer.

Asset Values

The land and buildings, for all except the Bremer Division, are carried at $875,000 (net of depreciation) in the balance sheet. An appraisal made in December of 1967 showed a "fair cash value" for the land and buildings of $1,600,000. The sale of a small portion of the plant after the appraisal date indicates that the appraisal values are realistic. A current appraisal of most of the machinery and equipment shows that the carrying values of these items could be realized upon disposition.

The investments are carried at cost on the balance sheet and evidence indicates these could be disposed of at a small gain. Receivables and inventories, other than those discussed above, are fairly stated.

Pending Litigation

Various suits exceeding $1,000,000 in the aggregate were pending against the company. Counsel for the company considered most of these claims to be without basis and estimated the eventual loss to be of no major consequence. The ultimate effect of these claims, however, could not be determined. Other than this, the liabilities of the company were fairly stated as of June 30, 1970.

In preparing the financial statements as of June 30, 1970, management of the company disclosed the pending litigation, the decline in sales and the operating losses of the Bremer Division but did not disclose the estimated loss on disposition of the Division because a decision had not yet been made to discontinue its operations.

Issues for consideration:

(1) What type of opinion should the auditors issue on the statements taken as a whole as of June 30, 1970? Discuss reasons for the type of opinion proposed.

(2) In case a disclaimer or an adverse opinion is issued, should a piecemeal opinion be issued on individual items in the financial statement? If so, what items and why?

(3) What disclosure should be made of the appraisal value of the plant and equipment? Of the suits pending?

(4) With regard to generally accepted accounting principles, discuss the relationship between the probable loss on the receivables and inventories and the appraisal increment on the plant. Should the "loss" on the former be offset by the "gain" on the latter? Discuss. Do you detect any inconsistency in generally accepted accounting principles on this issue?

Rainbow Manufacturing Co., Inc.

Rainbow Manufacturing Co., Inc., is a large-scale manufacturer and distributor of specialty furniture and equipment for office and other commercial uses. Rainbow products are sold on a nation-wide basis and its level of sales approaches $100,000,000 per year. The stock of Rainbow is traded on a national exchange.

During the year ended October 31, 1971, Rainbow undertook an extensive review of its depreciation policy. As a result, Rainbow's controller recommended that the useful lives of most of the company's property and equipment be increased and that the company adopt the straight-line method of depreciation for all of its depreciable assets. The company has been using accelerated depreciation for both tax and book purposes since 1962. The controller felt that Rainbow should continue to use the accelerated depreciation method in its tax return. The changes recommended would put Rainbow on a more comparable basis with other firms in the industry and the controller further argued that the changes would make the financial statements more realistic for the stockholders.

After a discussion with its auditors, Rainbow decided to adopt on a prospective basis the recommendations of the controller. The effect of the changes for the year ended October 31, 1971, both of which increased net income, was as follows:

Effect of Change in Method of Depreciation (Net of taxes)	$ 880,000
Effect of Change in Useful Lives (Net of taxes)	1,460,000

Net income for the year was $8,696,000 after giving effect to the changes. Net income for the year ended October 31, 1970, as previously reported, was $8,101,000.

These changes were covered in the following note to the financial statements:

Effective November 1, 1970, the Company, for financial reporting purposes, changed from an accelerated method to the straight-line method of computing depreciation while continuing to use accelerated methods for tax purposes. In addition, the lives used in computing depreciation for most of its property and equipment were increased from an average of 15 years to 20 years. As a result of these changes, net income for the year ended October 31, 1971, was increased by $2,340,000 or $ .17 a share.

Although comparative statements for 1970 and 1971 were furnished, no attempt was made to restate the 1970 statements on a retroactive basis.

The auditors decided to qualify their opinion on the 1971 statements as to consistency but referred only to the change in the method of depreciation.

Issues for consideration:

(1) Do you agree with the auditors' decision in this instance? Why or why not?
(2) What type of opinion should the auditors have issued under the circumstances?
(3) Should firms adopting a change in the method of computing depreciation be required to reflect the change retroactively? Explain.
(4) What would your position have been if the company had changed the asset lives but not the method of depreciation?

The Millcraft Manufacturing Company

The Millcraft Manufacturing Company was organized in the early 1950's to fabricate equipment for the oil and gas exploration industry. By 1970 the company's sales reached a level of $1.5 million and assets exceeded $10 million.

In October 1970 Mr. L. G. Moore, president and part owner of Millcraft, engaged the auditing firm of Thatcher, Reynard & Co. to conduct an examination of its financial statements as of December 31, 1970. Millcraft had not been audited prior to 1970; however, the management felt that in view of its plan for securing additional funds, the company should be audited by independent auditors.

In conducting the audit, Thatcher, Reynard & Co. found several deficiencies in Millcraft's accounting records. Since its organization, Millcraft has followed the practice of using its own facilities and personnel to construct many of its own machines as well as most of its buildings. Sixty percent of the machinery and equipment and forty percent of the company's buildings were self-constructed assets; however, no record was found of any overhead having been charged to such assets. Management's estimates revealed that overhead would have represented 40% to 50% of total costs; however, accounting records were inadequate to reconstruct these costs with any degree of accuracy.

No detailed property records were maintained and the auditors were unable to find documentary support for most material and labor charges. A summary of the financial statements of Millcraft showed the following:

December 31, 1970

Current Assets	$ 3,872,000
Investments	244,000
Machinery and Equipment (Net)	4,266,000
Buildings (Net)	737,000
Land	700,000
Other Assets	349,000
Total Assets	$10,168,000

Current Liabilities	$ 3,877,000
Long-Term Debt	3,690,000
Other Liabilities	140,000
Stockholders' Equity	2,461,000
Total Equities	$10,168,000

12 Months Ended December 31, 1970

Sales	$ 1,568,000
Cost of Sales	(1,042,000)
General and Administrative Expenses	(326,000)
Other Deductions	(112,000)
Net Income	$ 88,000

Financial statements as of December 31, 1969, were not presented because management felt they were completely unreliable in view of the deficiencies found by the auditors.

In preparing the audit report, Thatcher, Reynard & Co. used the standard wording in the scope paragraph. A middle paragraph was inserted which cited the auditors' lack of satisfaction with their examination of machinery, equipment and buildings.

Issues for consideration:

(1) What type of opinion paragraph would you recommend under the circumstances? Explain.

(2) What other changes, if any, would you make in the auditor's report?

(3) Under what circumstances, if any, would you approve an unqualified opinion for Millcraft Manufacturing Company? If the financial statements need to be adjusted, what types of adjustments would you recommend?

(4) If no additional deficiencies are uncovered in the subsequent year's audit, will an unqualified opinion be warranted?

Miro Royale Co., Ltd.

In October of 1970, the international accounting firm of Peet, Water & Rasken was engaged by International Company, Inc., to audit Miro Royale Co., Ltd., one of its foreign subsidiaries located in France. Miro, which had been acquired by International 15 years earlier, manufactures a widely accepted brand of household detergents and soaps. Miro's financial statements are included in the consolidated financial statements of International which have been audited by Peet, Water & Rasken in recent years. Due to the relative insignificance of Miro's financial statements in relation to the consolidated statements, the auditors had limited their work in prior years to the observation and pricing of inventories and other limited procedures.

Prior to 1970 Miro valued its inventories at standard costs with annual quantity variations priced on a LIFO basis. Standards had been studied carefully in 1965 and no substantive changes had been made since that time. In addition, Miro maintained an overall inventory reserve of $640,000. Miro's management had considered the reserve a symbol of prudent management and a hedge against excessive tax liabilities. Prior to the determination of the inventory at December 31, 1970, Miro decided to change the method of inventory valuation to direct costing. The change permitted the elimination of the inventory reserve but it did not have a material effect on the aggregate valuation of the inventory as compared to the earlier method. Consequently, the effect of this decision on net income for the year was minimal.

After consultation with the auditors, Miro attached the following note to its financial statements:

> During 1970, the company changed the method of valuing inventory from standard cost using LIFO to price quantity variances, less an additional valuation reserve of $640,000, to the direct costing method using current standards for material, labor, and variable overhead. The change had no material effect on the carrying value of the inventory or on the net income for the year as compared with the method previously used by the company.

The auditors determined that if the company had adopted the full absorption costing method, the inventories as of December 31, 1970, would have been increased by $1.5 million.

A part of the financial data for Miro appears below:

December 31, 1970

Inventories (At direct standard cost)	$ 6,230,000
Total Current Assets	12,788,000
Total Assets	37,233,000
Capital Stock and Surplus	15,981,000

12 Months Ended December 31, 1970

Sales	$29,405,000
Net Income	1,322,000

Issues for consideration:

(1) Discuss the crucial issues which are raised in the set of circumstances described above. If audit report qualifications are called for, what should they be and how should they be reported by the auditor?

(2) If the company had not changed its method of valuing inventory for 1970, would a qualification have been required in the audit report? Comment.

(3) Under what circumstances, if any, would the use of direct costing permit the issuance of an unqualified audit report? Comment.

Consistency of Application of Accounting Principles

Generally accepted auditing standards require that the audit report state whether accounting principles have been consistently applied in the current period in relation to the preceding period. According to Statement No. 33, the objective of the consistency standard is:

(1) To give assurance that the comparability of financial statements as between periods has not been materially affected by changes in the accounting principles employed or in the method of their application; or

(2) If comparability has been materially affected by such changes, to require a statement of the nature of the changes and their effects on the financial statements.

Lack of comparability of financial statements as between years is generally caused by one of the following conditions:

(1) A change in accounting principles employed. Examples are a change from the completed-contract method to the percentage-of-completion method and a change from the FIFO inventory method to the LIFO method. Reference should be made to Chapter 10 of Accounting Research Study No. 7 for additional examples.

(2) Changed conditions which necessitate accounting changes but which do not involve changes in the accounting principles employed. Examples are a change in the estimated useful lives of fixed assets and a change in consolidation practices when a parent company acquires a dissimilar company, such as a manufacturing company acquiring a finance company.

(3) Changed conditions unrelated to accounting. Examples are the disposition of a branch and the issuance of bonds.

Statement No. 33 states that only condition (1) above involves the consistency standard. The other types of changes cited do not require disclosure in the auditor's report but footnote disclosure may be desirable in order to assure fair presentation of financial statements.

The cases in this section involve circumstances in which the comparability of the financial statements is at issue. Other reporting problems are also involved in most of the cases in this section. The reader should utilize Chapter 8 of Statement No. 33 as a reference in analyzing these cases.

American Industries, Inc.

American Industries, Inc., manufactures, distributes, and services air-conditioning and heating systems for residential and commercial customers. Through one of its divisions, American also does installation work on a contract basis, primarily for commercial customers. The time required for each installation ranges from a few days to several months. American's share of the installation market has been increasing and management expectations are for larger and longer term contracts in the future.

The company has always used the completed-contract method of accounting for its installation work. However, in 1970 the company's independent public accountants, Steady & Sharpe, made a comprehensive review of the company's accounting procedures and recommended to management that the percentage-of-completion method be adopted for purposes of reporting to management and stockholders. Steady & Sharpe advised management that the percentage-of-completion method would produce a more relevant income figure. The fluctuation in earnings due to the timing of completion dates of major contracts would be eliminated. The accountants also explained that the tax reporting method need not be changed and any differences between the two methods could be accounted for by using the deferred income tax technique. Management agreed and the change was made effective for the year ended December 31, 1970.

The effect of the change on the 1970 statements is summarized as follows:

	As Reported	Without Change
1970 Total Revenue	$155,247,000	$143,381,000
1970 Net Income	13,894,000	12,909,000
Deferred Income Taxes Payable	893,000	

The company found that it was impractical to determine the effect of the change on the 1969 statements since detailed information on open contracts at December 31, 1968 and 1969 had not been maintained by the accounting department. However, American's controller was able to develop an estimate which showed the effect to be about $7.5 million on 1969 sales and $420,000 on net income for 1969.

The company gave a full explanation of the change in a footnote to the financial statements. An excerpt from the footnote explaining the change read as follows:

In 1970, the company changed the method of accounting for its contracting operations from the completed-contract to the percentage-of-completion method. Under the percentage-of-completion method, income is recognized as contract work progresses rather than when the contract is completed. As a result of the adoption of the percentage-of-completion method, total revenues for 1970 are $11,866,000 more than the amount which would have been reported under the previously used completed-contract method. Also, net income for 1970 was increased by $985,000 or $ .12 per share.

Upon completion of the regular audit work for the year ended December 31, 1970, Steady & Sharpe prepared the audit report.

Issues for consideration:

(1) What type of audit report should the independent accountants have issued in the above situation? Why?

(2) Would you have taken a different position if the effect of the change on net income had been $1.5 million? How would you have worded your opinion paragraph in this case?

(3) If American had not provided for deferred income taxes, how would this have affected your audit report? How should this item be classified on the balance sheet?

(4) Would you question the soundness of the change recommended by the independent accountants? Comment.

(5) If the effect of the change to the percentage-of-completion method is not considered material with respect to the financial statements of the current year, what influence should the probable future effect of the change have on the auditors' considerations? Explain.

Western Fabricators, Inc.

Western Fabricators, Inc., is located in Denver and is engaged in the manufacture and assembly of medicine cabinets, sliding doors, and windows for the construction industry.

Although the company had used the LIFO inventory method for several years, in 1970 management decided to install a comprehensive cost accounting system which required the use of the average cost method of pricing the inventory. Management directed that the balance sheet as of December 31, 1970, and the income statement for the year 1970 be prepared to reflect the average cost method. The change was designed to improve the usefulness of the financial reports to management and, in the long run, enhance substantially the company's working capital position.

The effect of the change on the 1970 financial statements may be summarized as follows:

	As Reported	Without Change
Net Income	$1,460,000	$1,370,000
Inventories	3,280,000	3,120,000

The note to the financial statements explaining the change in the method of pricing inventories pointed out that the change did not have a material effect on inventories at December 31, 1970, and would not have had a material effect on beginning inventories if applied to such inventories.

The auditor's report on Western Fabricators' financial statements as of December 31, 1970, contained the usual wording except for a portion of the opinion paragraph, which read as follows:

> . . . with generally accepted accounting principles which, other than for the change (which we approve) to the average method of determining inventory costs as indicated in Note 3 to the financial statements, were applied on a basis consistent with that of the preceding year.

Western Fabricators reported net income of $1,250,000 for the year 1969. Inventories at the end of 1969 were reported at $3,100,000 and total assets at that time were $18,370,000.

Issues for consideration:

(1) Should the auditor have qualified the opinion as shown above? Why or why not?

(2) What are the responsibilities of the auditor for assessing the future consequences of changes in the application of accounting principles? What should be the limits of his responsibility?

Astrodyne Development Corp.

Alcorn & Meade, a national public accounting firm, audits the financial statements of National Aircraft, Inc. National, which is one of the largest manufacturers of commercial and military aircraft, planned to acquire the assets and liabilities of Astrodyne Development Corp. by the issuance of common stock. As a result of the proposed acquisition, National engaged Alcorn & Meade to examine the balance sheet of Astrodyne as of July 31, 1970, and the income statement for the nine months ended July 31, 1970.

Astrodyne manufactures electro-optics instruments and sensing devices under contracts with the United States government and private firms in the aviation industry. Until October 31, 1969, the end of its previous fiscal year, Astrodyne had followed the practice of reporting income on all of its fixed-fee contracts on a completed-contract basis. Cost-plus-fixed-fee contracts were reported on a percentage-of-completion basis, but these did not account for a material portion of Astrodyne's business. In January, 1970, Astrodyne secured a contract from the National Aeronautics and Space Administration for optics systems under a fixed-fee type arrangement. The contract price was in excess of $5,000,000, which was substantially greater than any contract Astrodyne had ever negotiated. The time required to complete the contract was expected to be about eighteen months.

Due to the size of the NASA contract, it became clear that the results of operations for the nine months ended July 31, 1970, would be distorted if the completed-contract method were applied to the NASA contract. After consultation with the auditors, Astrodyne decided to change the method of reporting income to the percentage-of-completion basis on the NASA contract. The accounting method for other fixed-fee contracts was not changed; however, an analysis did show that income would not have been materially affected if percentage-of-completion had been used for all contracts on a retroactive basis.

As a result of the change, the company reported $2,700,000 of contract costs and $3,150,000 of contract revenue attributable to the NASA contract during the period ended July 31, 1970. Relevant data for the nine months ended July 31, 1970, were as follows:

Revenues $6,800,000
Net Income 312,000

The auditors recommended that the company also adopt the percentage-of-completion method for all fixed-fee contracts. The company rejected this recommendation; however, management did agree to disclose fully the effects of the NASA contract in the notes to the financial statements.

Issues for consideration:

(1) Should the auditors qualify their report? Give reasons for your answer.
(2) What wording would you suggest for the opinion paragraph?
(3) Do you agree with the auditors' proposal that all fixed-fee contracts be accounted for by the percentage-of-completion method?

Decker Sportsman Supply Co.

Decker Sportsman Supply Co. manufactures a line of fishing supplies. Its tackle and fishing lures are sold in national markets.

Decker owns 100% of the stock of RGT Corp., and until 1970 RGT's financial statements have been consolidated with Decker's. During the year ended September 30, 1970, RGT Corp., which manufactures molded plastic fishing rods and reels, operated at a substantial loss. Summary data from Decker's financial statements (unconsolidated) appear below:

September 30, 1970

Current Assets	$ 6,458,000
Fixed Assets (Net)	3,490,000
Investment in RGT Corp. and Other Assets	1,654,000
Total Assets	$11,602,000
Current Liabilities	$ 4,134,000
Long-Term Debt	1,210,000
Stockholders' Equity	6,258,000
Total Equities	$11,602,000

12 Months Ended September 30, 1970

Sales	$13,614,000
Income from Operations	$ 1,226,000
Other Expense (Including operating loss of RGT Corp. of $439,000)	669,000
Income before Extraordinary Loss	$ 557,000
Write-down of Investment in RGT Corp. to Estimated Realizable Value (Less income tax benefits)	285,000
Net Income	$ 272,000

After a careful evaluation of RGT's potential, management decided to liquidate its investment in RGT in December 1970. Management estimated that an additional loss of about $285,000, net of income taxes, would be incurred on the liquidation. The company's independent auditors recommended that the investment in RGT be shown at the estimated net realizable value on the balance sheet as of September 30, 1970, and that the estimated loss on its liquidation be reflected in the related income statement as well as the loss from its operations for fiscal 1970. Furthermore, in order to make the financial statements comparable, the auditors suggested that the statements of 1969 be restated to conform to the approach used in 1970.

Decker's financial statements were prepared on the basis recommended by the auditors and a footnote contained an explanation of the change in the method of accounting for the subsidiary and the reason for this change.

Issues for consideration:

(1) Should the auditors include a consistency qualification in the opinion on the financial statements as of September 30, 1970? Why or why not?

(2) Give the wording of the audit report which should be issued in this case.

(3) Do the circumstances described above constitute a change in the application of accounting principles or a change in conditions, or both?

(4) What would your position be if the subsidiary had net income of $439,000 for the year ended September 30, and management estimated a gain on liquidation of $285,000?

Universal Controls Corp.

Universal Controls Corp. is a midwest-based company engaged in the manufacture and sale of automatic control devices. Because its products are gaining a national reputation for quality, the company greatly increased its sales volume from 1969 to 1971.

In 1970, for the first time, Universal had its financial statements audited by the Denver office of a national public accounting firm. Prior to this time the company had always used a local CPA firm to assist it in the preparation of its income tax returns based on unaudited financial statements. Upon the completion of their audit for 1970, the auditors issued an unqualified opinion on the balance sheet at December 31, 1970, but disclaimed an opinion on the statement of income and retained earnings for the year because of their failure to observe or to use other means to satisfy themselves as to the beginning inventory. Management's desire to minimize the cost of the audit was the principal reason for the limitation in the auditors' examination of the beginning inventory.

At the end of 1971 the accounting firm again conducted an audit of Universal. The 1971 financial statements of Universal were found to be fairly presented and in conformity with generally accepted accounting principles. A question did arise, however, concerning the propriety of expressing an opinion as to the consistency of application of accounting principles in 1971 compared to the previous year when a disclaimer had been issued on the statement of income and retained earnings for the prior year.

Issues for consideration:

(1) What position would you take? Why?
(2) How would you word the opinion paragraph on the 1971 financial statements?
(3) Would you change your position if the disclaimer in 1970 resulted from a failure to carry out certain tests of accounting procedures?

The Industrial Security Co.

The Industrial Security Co. is engaged in providing protective services to industrial firms and governmental agencies. The company maintains a large inventory of guard uniforms and supplies, thus permitting it to expand its work force on short notice. The company has been growing steadily in recent years and, accordingly, its inventory has increased significantly.

Industrial Security had, until 1970, amortized all uniforms and supplies over a two-year basis. However, in 1970 the bank that finances the company's inventories requested that the company have its financial statements audited by a CPA firm. In preparing for the audit, the company had its stockroom manager review the operating experience with respect to its guard uniforms. This review revealed that most uniforms were used for four years or more; many of the related items of supply were in use for a period of four to six years. As a result of the review, Industrial Security decided to change to a four-year amortization policy on uniforms and supplies and to make the change retroactive to 1968. The change affected net income previously reported as summarized below:

Year Ended December 31	Previously Reported	Increase
1968	$ 477,000	$ 44,600
1969	553,000	61,800

The net income reported for 1970 was $619,000 and the inventory on December 31 was $278,300. The audited financial statements for 1970 contained a note which explained the retroactive change.

Issues for consideration:

(1) As auditor for Industrial Security, what effect would the change adopted by Industrial Security have on your report?

(2) Is materiality of the effect of the change a crucial issue to the auditor in this case? Why or why not?

(3) What type of change did Industrial Security make in 1970 as defined by Statement No. 33?

(4) Distinguish between a change which involves consistency of application of accounting principles and one which involves changed conditions.

Peerless Company, Inc.

Peerless Company, Inc., is a major contractor providing weapons systems and weapons technology to the United States government. During 1970, 60% of its output went to the United States government and 40% went to private industry.

Peerless has the reputation of being one of the most successful contractors in the weapons area. However, during 1969 and 1970 Peerless was experiencing a profit squeeze as a result of rising labor costs and high interest rates.

Included below are summarized data from the financial statements of Peerless.

	December 31	
	1969	1970
Cash and Marketable Securities	$ 12,500,000	$ 10,850,000
Accounts Receivable (Government)	34,400,000	37,620,000
Accounts Receivable (Others)	12,120,000	14,300,000
Inventories (At cost not in excess of net realizable value)	48,150,000	53,410,000
Plant and Equipment (Net)	45,600,000	43,880,000
Other Assets	9,420,000	8,670,000
Total Assets	$162,190,000	$168,730,000
Current Liabilities	$ 74,930,000	$ 81,140,000
Long-Term Debt	15,400,000	11,400,000
Stockholders' Equity	71,860,000	76,190,000
Total Equities	$162,190,000	$168,730,000

	12 Months Ended	
	Dec. 31, 1969	Dec. 31, 1970
Revenues	$304,430,000	$297,260,000
Cost and Expenses	286,870,000	285,380,000
Net Income	$ 17,560,000	$ 11,880,000
Per Share	$4.28	$2.90

In developing the complex weapons systems for the government, Peerless must develop and test the weapons component over a long period of time. Profit on each contract is taken into income as deliveries are made under each contract.

Prior to 1970 research and development costs, direct tooling and production costs, and applicable administrative and general expenses on weapons under development were charged to expense as incurred.

In 1970 the management of Peerless decided to charge all of the afore-mentioned developmental costs to work in process. As a result of these changes in accounting procedures the earnings for 1970 were increased by $5.3 million or $1.29 per share. The changes were not made retroactive to 1969; however, notes to the financial statements contained a full explanation of the changes and their effect. The notes cited prevailing practice in the industry as one of the reasons for the changes by management.

For income tax purposes, Peerless continued to deduct all developmental costs on its weapons systems as incurred and thus reported deferred income taxes of $5.25 million as a current liability.

At the completion of its regular annual audit for 1970, the auditing firm of Wilson & Row issued the report shown below:

We have examined the accompanying consolidated balance sheet of Peerless Company, Inc., and subsidiaries at December 31, 1970, and the related consolidated statement of earnings for the year then ended. Our examination was made in accordance with generally accepted auditing standards, and accordingly included such tests of the accounting records and such other auditing procedures as we considered necessary in the circumstances. It was not practicable to confirm certain amounts included in receivables from the United States government, as to which we satisfied ourselves by means of other auditing procedures.

In our opinion, the statements mentioned above present fairly the consolidated financial position of Peerless Company, Inc., and its subsidiaries at December 31, 1970, and the consolidated results of their operations for the year then ended, in conformity with generally accepted accounting principles applied on a basis consistent with that of the preceding year except for the change in accounting for developmental costs described in Note 1.

Issues for consideration:

(1) Is the wording of the auditor's report appropriate under the circumstances? Explain any change you would recommend.
(2) Is the deferral of developmental costs on inventories in process an acceptable accounting procedure? Defend your answer.
(3) Should the change in the costing of inventories be made retroactive to 1969? Why or why not?

United States Steel Corporation

United States Steel Corporation is the nation's largest and most dominant company in the steel industry. Raw steel produced during 1968 totaled 32.4 million tons compared to 30.9 million tons in 1967.

The recorded cost of United States Steel's physical facilities at December 31, 1968, was $8.6 billion and the cost of wear and exhaustion of facilities during 1968 was $256 million. Effective for the year 1968, United States Steel, for financial reporting purposes, revised the lives of certain properties and changed from accelerated methods of computing depreciation to the straight-line method. In addition, the investment credit for 1968 was taken directly into income of that year while the investment credit for prior years continues to be allocated to future periods, including 1968. These changes resulted in an increase of $94 million in the reported net income for the year 1968.

The following 5 pages show the published financial statements and notes of United States Steel Corporation and the auditor's report on such statements.

Issues for consideration:

(1) Discuss the probable reasons for the changes explained in the notes to financial statements entitled "Wear and Exhaustion of Facilities."

(2) Should changes to acceptable alternative accounting methods which cause a material change in income be made on a retroactive basis including a restatement of all prior years' financial statements presented? Comment.

(3) The United States Steel annual report gives the "Summary of 1968 Financial Operations" equal status with the Statement of Income and the Statement of Financial Position. However, only the latter two statements are covered by the auditors' report. Comment.

Financial Statements
Summary of 1968 Financial Operations

ADDITIONS TO WORKING CAPITAL

Income	$ 253,675,549
Add—Wear and exhaustion of facilities	253,114,609
Deferred taxes on income	85,781,057
Reclassification of deferred taxes on income accrued in prior years	86,505,000
Proceeds from sales and salvage of plant and equipment	8,530,687
Increase in total long-term debt, less payments of $63,862,497	371,220,156
Total additions	1,058,827,058

DEDUCTIONS FROM WORKING CAPITAL

Expended for plant and equipment	$697,368,858	
Dividends declared on common stock	129,947,699	
Miscellaneous deductions	11,424,610	
Total deductions		838,741,167
INCREASE IN WORKING CAPITAL		$ 220,085,891

WORKING CAPITAL PER CONSOLIDATED STATEMENT
OF FINANCIAL POSITION

December 31, 1968	$875,321,122	
December 31, 1967	655,235,231	
INCREASE		$ 220,085,891

Consolidated Statement of
Income

	1968	1967
PRODUCTS AND SERVICES SOLD	$4,609,234,734	$4,067,227,425
COSTS		
Employment costs		
Wages and salaries	1,734,019,614	1,587,584,702
Employe benefits *(see page 18)*	321,897,182	284,061,968
	2,055,916,796	1,871,646,670
Products and services bought	1,766,144,174	1,431,838,466
Wear and exhaustion of facilities	253,114,609	354,705,686
Interest and other costs on long-term debt	67,043,333	54,394,067
State, local and miscellaneous taxes	113,340,273	106,162,955
Estimated United States and foreign taxes on income	100,000,000	76,000,000
Total	4,355,559,185	3,894,747,844
INCOME	253,675,549	172,479,581
Income Per Common Share	$4.69	$3.19
DIVIDENDS DECLARED		
On common stock *($2.40 per share)*	129,947,699	129,943,814
INCOME REINVESTED IN BUSINESS	$ 123,727,850	$ 42,535,767

CASE NO. 23

Consolidated Statement of Financial Position

	Dec. 31, 1968	Dec. 31, 1967
CURRENT ASSETS		
Cash	$ 268,023,799	$ 268,073,369
Marketable securities, at cost (approximates market)	461,825,000	162,686,870
Receivables, less estimated bad debts	467,189,236	398,496,401
Inventories *(details on page 25)*	813,530,008	842,788,342
Total	2,010,568,043	1,672,044,982
Less		
CURRENT LIABILITIES		
Notes and accounts payable	834,171,442	626,555,154
Accrued taxes	247,218,768	337,094,746
Dividend payable	32,488,417	32,486,363
Long-term debt due within one year	21,368,294	20,673,488
Total	1,135,246,921	1,016,809,751
WORKING CAPITAL	875,321,122	655,235,231
Marketable securities, at cost (approximates market), set aside for property additions and replacements	655,000,000	655,000,000
Other investments, at cost less estimated losses	147,415,216	134,331,105
Plant and equipment, less depreciation *(details on page 25)*	3,446,030,129	3,010,306,567
Operating parts and supplies	51,973,773	51,504,865
Costs applicable to future periods	80,346,897	83,123,256
TOTAL ASSETS LESS CURRENT LIABILITIES	5,256,087,137	4,589,501,024
Deduct		
Long-term debt *(details on page 25)*	1,571,255,675	1,200,730,325
Reserves and deferred taxes on income *(details on page 25)* . . .	340,349,303	168,054,640
EXCESS OF ASSETS OVER LIABILITIES AND RESERVES	$3,344,482,159	$3,220,716,059
OWNERSHIP EVIDENCED BY		
Common stock (authorized 90,000,000 shares; outstanding 54,145,212 shares at December 31, 1968 and 54,143,937 shares at December 31, 1967)		
Par value $30 per share	$1,624,356,360	$1,624,318,110
Income reinvested in business	1,720,125,799	1,596,397,949
(see page 23 for addition of $123,727,850 in 1968)		
Total	$3,344,482,159	$3,220,716,059

Notes to
Financial Statements

PRINCIPLES APPLIED IN CONSOLIDATION

Subsidiaries consolidated include all companies (with minor exceptions) of which a majority of the capital stock is owned by U. S. Steel or by any of its consolidated subsidiaries.

STOCK OPTION INCENTIVE PLANS

The Stock Option Incentive Plan approved by stockholders in 1964 and the Plan approved in 1951 authorized the option and sale of up to 1,500,000 shares and 2,600,000 shares of common stock, respectively, to key management employes, such shares of stock to be made available from authorized unissued or reacquired common stock at market price on the date the options are granted. An option may be exercised in whole at any time, or in part from time to time, during the option period if no prior option is outstanding at a higher price. The option period begins on the date the option is granted and ends five years (1964 Plan) and ten years (1951 Plan) thereafter, except in cases of death, retirement or other earlier termination.

In 1968, options for 530,775 shares were granted to 230 employes at the then market price of $39.625 per share. During 1968, 4 optionees purchased 1,275 shares at $36.75 per share under options granted under the 1964 Plan.

At December 31, 1968, 325 optionees held options to purchase 1,468,625 shares at prices ranging from $36.75 to $82.00 per share for a total of $64.5 million and 35,100 shares were available for future options.

SECURITIES SET ASIDE FOR PROPERTY ADDITIONS AND REPLACEMENTS

At December 31, 1968, completion of authorized additions to and replacements of facilities required an estimated further expenditure of $1,110 million and marketable securities set aside to cover in part such authorized expenditures totaled $655 million, the same as at the end of 1967.

WEAR AND EXHAUSTION OF FACILITIES

For the most part, wear and exhaustion of facilities is related to U. S. Steel's rate of operations and is based on the guideline procedures established in 1962 by the Internal Revenue Service.

Effective for the year 1968, U. S. Steel, for financial reporting purposes, revised the lives of certain properties and changed from accelerated methods of computing depreciation to the straight-line method. The 1968 investment credit provided for in the income tax laws has been taken directly into income as a reduction in the provision for income taxes; the investment credit for 1967 and prior years continues to be allocated to future years; the amounts included in 1968 income totaled $38.6 million. After provision for deferred taxes on income, the depreciation and investment credit changes resulted in increased income of $94.0 million.

RESERVES AND DEFERRED TAXES ON INCOME

U. S. Steel is, for the most part, a self-insurer of its assets against fire, windstorm, marine and related losses. The insurance reserve of $50 million is held available for absorbing possible losses of this character, and is considered adequate for this purpose.

The reserves for contingencies and accident and hospital expenses of $50.1 million, provided mainly in previous years by charges to operations, are held for exceptional unanticipated losses other than those covered by the insurance reserve.

PREFERRED STOCK

At the Annual Meeting held on May 6, 1968, stockholders of U. S. Steel voted to amend the Certificate of Incorporation to authorize the issuance of 20,000,000 shares of a new class of preferred stock, without par value. At December 31, 1968, none of this stock had been issued.

PENSION FUNDING

U. S. Steel's pension plan covers substantially all its employes. Pension costs are determined by an independent actuary, based upon various actuarial factors and an actuarial method under which both current and unfunded past service costs are funded over the future on a combined basis by payment into pension trusts. For 1968, the cost of pensions amounted to $70.2 million compared with $65.4 million in 1967.

The combined assets of the contributory and noncontributory pension trusts were $1,965.2 million at December 31, 1968 and $1,869.6 million at December 31, 1967, as set forth in the statement appearing on page 30. These funds are held by the trustee,

CASE NO. 23

Independent Auditors' Report

(Notes to Financial Statements continued)

United States Steel and Carnegie Pension Fund (a non-profit Pennsylvania membership corporation), solely for the payment of benefits under the U. S. Steel pension plan.

OTHER ITEMS

Other Investments — Other investments include long-term receivables of $84.1 million.

Production Payments — In December 1968, U. S. Steel sold proceeds of mineral production payments which represent an interest in a portion of future production of minerals. These transactions are reflected in operations over the lives of the contracts.

Products and Services Sold—Products and services sold includes interest, dividends and other income of $72.5 million in 1968 and $61.7 million in 1967.

Costs—Wages and salaries totaled $1,767.2 million in 1968 of which $1,734.0 million was included in costs of products and services sold and the balance was charged to construction.

Products and services bought reflects the changes during the year in inventories and deferred costs. These items decreased during 1968 approximately $32 million.

If the total of wages and salaries and products and services bought in 1968 were reclassified as costs of products and services sold and general administrative and selling expenses, the amounts thereof would be $3,295.8 million and $204.3 million, respectively.

Maintenance and repairs of plant and equipment totaled $639.5 million in 1968.

Non-cancellable charters and leases covering ore ships, office space, and other properties with minimum rentals aggregating approximately $38 million per year were in effect at December 31, 1968, the major portion of which terminates within ten years. In 1968, expenditures on such charters and leases amounted to approximately $46 million.

PRICE WATERHOUSE & CO.

60 BROAD STREET

NEW YORK 10004

February 25, 1969

To the Stockholders of

United States Steel Corporation:

In our opinion, the accompanying Consolidated Statement of Financial Position and related Statement of Income present fairly the position of United States Steel Corporation and subsidiaries at December 31, 1968 and the results of operations for the year, in conformity with generally accepted accounting principles. These principles were applied on a basis consistent with that of the preceding year, except for the changes, which we approve, in the methods of computing depreciation and accounting for the investment credit as described in the note, "Wear and Exhaustion of Facilities." Our examination of these statements was made in accordance with generally accepted auditing standards and accordingly included such tests of the accounting records and such other auditing procedures as we considered necessary in the circumstances.

Price Waterhouse & Co.

Existence of Unusual Uncertainties in Financial Statements

The financial statements contain measurements which reflect management's evaluation of future developments. In instances where the probable effects of future events are not reasonably determinable and where the outcome will depend on the decision of parties other than management, the auditor should qualify his opinion.

When unusual uncertainties exist, the auditor uses the phrase "subject to" in the opinion paragraph of the audit report, whereas in other instances which call for a qualification, the auditor uses the phrase "except for."

In instances where the magnitude of the effects of the uncertainty is material and the probability of an unfavorable outcome is high, the auditor should disclaim an opinion on the financial statements taken as a whole. Further, where an uncertainty or contingency exists, the auditor should not issue an unqualified opinion unless the management of the company or its legal counsel makes a direct representation that, in its opinion, any loss would not have a material effect on the statements. The auditor must, of course, be satisfied that there is a reasonable basis for the company's position.

The cases in this section were selected to demonstrate some of the complex situations which the auditor faces in assessing the impact of uncertainty on financial statements.

Alcord Company, Inc.

Alcord Company, Inc., is a closely-held company engaged in the pipeline supply business. In May of 1970 Alcord encountered working capital problems and arranged to borrow $3,500,000 from a local bank at 8% on a long-term basis. As security the company gave a mortgage on its real property and pledged all equipment, inventory, and receivables. The loan agreement contained several restrictions and limitations and provided that, in the event of failure to comply with the provisions of the loan agreement, the bank, at its option, could declare the note to be immediately due and payable.

The loan agreement with the bank contained the following restrictions:

(1) The debtor company shall maintain a working capital ratio of 2 to 1 at all times. In the event of failure to maintain the said ratio the company shall restrict annual compensation of officers to a total of $150,000.

(2) The debtor company shall maintain an amount of working capital such that at all times the working capital shall be equal to at least 50% of the total of all long-term debt.

(3) The debtor company shall keep all property which is security for this debt insured against loss by fire and other natural hazards to the extent of 100% of its actual value.

(4) The debtor company shall pay all taxes legally assessed against all property which is security for this loan within the time provided by law for such payment.

(5) The debtor company shall not engage in additional long-term borrowings and shall not grant any lien on the property of the company while this loan is in force.

During the examination of Alcord's financial statements as of December 31, 1970, the auditors, Tucker & Reece, noted that the company had occasionally failed to maintain a 2 to 1 working capital ratio and further noted that on November 1, 1970, the working capital was only 45% of long-term debt. In addition, Alcord's insurance coverage on its equipment was only 80% of actual value. Tucker & Reece approached the management of Alcord and suggested that they request a waiver of default from the bank. Management agreed and several meetings were held between the company and the bank.

At the date of the auditors' report, March 15, 1971, a waiver had not been issued and it did not appear likely that one would be issued soon. As of that date, however, the bank had not taken any formal action to call the loan.

Summarized data from Alcord's financial statements appear below:

December 31, 1970

Current Assets	$4,758,000
Fixed Assets (Net)	4,009,000
Other Assets	449,000
Total Assets	$9,216,000
Current Liabilities	$2,326,000
Long-Term Debt	4,200,000
Capital Stock	2,850,000
Retained Earnings (Deficit)	(160,000)
Total Liabilities and Stockholders' Equity	$9,216,000

12 Months Ended December 31, 1970

Sales	$7,294,000
Net Loss	285,000

A note attached to the financial statements read in part as follows:

At certain times during 1970 and at December 31, 1970, the Company was not in compliance with certain provisions of the loan agreement executed in May 1970 pertaining to the $3.5 million loan. The bank has been informed of the noncompliance; however, no indication has been received from the bank of what action, if any, will be taken.

Issues for consideration:

(1) What type of opinion should Tucker & Reece issue under the circumstances? Explain fully.

(2) Would your audit report differ if Alcord decided to reclassify the loan as a current debt? Explain.

Interstate Developers, Inc.

Interstate Developers, Inc., is a broadly diversified company owning improved and unimproved real estate, royalties in oil and gas properties, and major interests in several industrial parks and shopping centers. The majority interest in Interstate's outstanding common stock is held by one family, which also owns a major mortgage financing enterprise. About 45% of the stock of Interstate is widely held and traded on a local exchange in the Midwest.

In 1969 the Internal Revenue Service initiated a review of the income tax returns of Interstate for the fiscal years 1967 through 1969. By September 30, 1970, the year-end date, the Internal Revenue agent had not issued his report on Interstate. Informal conversations did reveal, however, that the agent was planning to challenge several items, which, if sustained, would result in a material deficiency assessment against Interstate.

Interstate's management asked its auditors, Hobson, Branson & Co., to assist in negotiations with the Service in addition to the regular audit. By the date of the audit's completion, Mr. Hobson, the partner in charge of the audit, attempted to assess the probable ultimate additional liability which might arise as a result of the agent's examination. A careful review of the agent's informal proposals (no written report had been issued) indicated that, although the total proposed assessment might be as much as $1.2 million, the probable maximum deficiency which the Service could sustain would approximate $407,000, including $35,000 for fiscal year 1970.

A condensed balance sheet and an income statement appear on the next page.

At year end Interstate's retained earnings were approximately $1,450,000. The stockholders were aware of company policy of not paying cash dividends. The market price of the stock (around $2 at September 30, 1970) seemed to be based to a great extent on the prospects of major appreciation in value of the company's real estate and industrial developments. A deficiency of $400,000 could have been readily satisfied with current funds; however, if the agent's total indicated claims were sustained, Interstate would have to arrange some long-term financing.

Balance Sheet
September 30, 1970

Current Assets	$ 4,883,000
Investments in Real Estate, Royalties, and Others	19,427,000
Long-Term Receivables and Advances	2,609,000
Other Assets	475,000
Total Assets	$27,394,000
Current Liabilities	$ 3,012,000
Long-Term Debt	4,400,000
Stockholders' Equity (15,000,000 shares of common stock)	19,982,000
Total Equities	$27,394,000

Income Statement
For 12 Months Ended September 30, 1970

Fees, Royalties, Gains, Etc.	$ 5,855,000
Deductions	5,599,000
Net Income	$ 256,000

Interstate's management objected to the inclusion of a footnote to the financial statements disclosing the amount of the probable additional tax liability. Management felt that the disclosure of an amount, even if less than the indicated proposals by the agent, would jeopardize their position and lend unnecessary support to the Service. After considerable discussion with the auditors, management consented to a footnote which informed the reader of the Internal Revenue Service examination and explained that the agent indicated that proposed deficiencies, if included in his report and sustained, would result in substantial additional tax liabilities. The footnote stressed the Company's plan to contest vigorously all proposed deficiencies and belief that the Service's examination would not result in material additional tax liabilities.

Issues for consideration:

(1) Should the auditors issue an unqualified opinion, a qualified opinion, or a disclaimer? Explain and defend your recommendation.

(2) If the financial statements had disclosed the total indicated proposed deficiency (per the agent) and management's estimate of the probable maximum deficiency, how would this affect the type of opinion you would recommend?

(3) Discuss the issue of materiality and the significance which this issue should have in the above described circumstance.

The Winslow Coal Co.

The Winslow Coal Co. is engaged in the business of mining, processing, and distributing coal from its holdings in eastern Kentucky. The company was organized in 1933 and, in spite of competition from larger companies with more modern equipment, has managed to continue operations throughout the years. However, since 1960, the company's earnings have dropped steadily and during 1969 and 1970 the company operated at a loss.

During 1970, the Blue Ridge Coal & Coke Co., a highly successful coal mining company, acquired 51% of the stock of Winslow for $317,000. At December 31, 1970, the book value of the interest acquired was $561,000. Blue Ridge considered the purchase price of the stock to be fair and attributed the excess of $244,000 value to the high-grade coal deposits owned by Winslow. Winslow's machinery and equipment are obsolete and grossly inefficient. Extensive replacement and renovation would be necessary to put the machinery and equipment in efficient operating condition. Most of the buildings were also in need of major repairs.

The auditing firm of Lindholm & Youngblood was called upon to audit the financial statements of Winslow for the year ended December 31, 1970. Summarized data from the balance sheet and income statement appear below:

December 31, 1970

Current Assets	$ 189,000
Buildings, Machinery and Equipment (Net)	283,000
Coal Deposits (Net)	848,000
Other Assets	14,000
Total Assets	$1,334,000
Current Liabilities	$ 177,000
Long-Term Debt	57,000
Capital Stock, Par Value $100	300,000
Paid-In Surplus	925,000
Retained Earnings (Deficit)	(125,000)
Total Equities	$1,334,000

12 Months Ended December 31, 1970

Sales		$ 591,000
Cost of Sales .... $ 497,000		
Selling and Administrative Exp. . . . 174,000		671,000
Net Loss		$ 80,000

Careful consideration was given to a major write-down of property values because of the substantial difference between the purchase price and the book value of the interest acquired, and the losses incurred during the last two years. The carrying value for the buildings acquired at the date of incorporation and the machinery and equipment then held had been determined by the Board of Directors. Winslow's management, after consultation with Blue Ridge, maintained that a write-down of the property was not called for at that time. Blue Ridge was optimistic that by lending its own technical know-how, the Winslow properties could be developed into profitable operations.

The following note was attached to the December 31, 1970, statements of Winslow:

During 1970, 51% of the company's capital stock was sold by the holders thereof to one buyer at a price of $317,000. At December 31, 1970, the book value of this portion of the capital stock was $561,000. Management, with the approval of the new majority stockholder, has decided not to make any adjustment to the carrying value of the company's assets until more experience has been gained under the new ownership.

Issues for consideration:

(1) Should the auditor render an opinion on the financial statements as a whole? If so, what type of opinion should be issued? Explain.

(2) Should a piecemeal opinion be issued? If so, what items would be considered fairly presented?

(3) If, during 1971, Winslow operated at a loss of $114,000, what difference would this fact make on your opinion for 1971 compared to your opinion for 1970? Explain.

Remrod Transit Corp.

Remrod Transit Corp. is a wholly owned subsidiary of National Transportation Co. Remrod was formed in 1963 to provide public transportation (buses) in an eastern seaboard city under an exclusive contract with the city council. This contract was subject to cancellation by the council at any time after a period of five years. Remrod's operations have never been successful. In addition, there was public pressure to terminate the contract due to general dissatisfaction with the quality of the bus service.

In its audit report dated September 1, 1969, on the financial statements of Remrod for the year ended June 30, 1969, the auditors, Kline & Keith, issued a qualified opinion in light of the uncertainty of the recovery of the investment in transportation equipment. Operations for the year ended June 30, 1969, showed a loss of $261,000.

By December 1969, the city council was under great pressure from the public to alter the provisions of its contract with Remrod or to terminate it entirely. On January 7, 1970, after a highly controversial hearing, the council voted to cancel the contract with Remrod.

In January 1970, Remrod's parent company belatedly realized that, as a result of the number of its shareholders exceeding 500, it was required to file a Form 10 Registration Statement with the Securities and Exchange Commission containing financial statements through June 30, 1969. Kline & Keith were requested to reissue their audit report on the financial statements of Remrod through June 30, 1969, since Remrod's statements were to become part of the consolidated statements required in the SEC registration statement which were to be reported on by other auditors.

Kline & Keith made a subsequent review for the period from September 1, 1969, (the date used in the last audit report) to February 1, 1970, (the date the SEC registration statement was filed).

Issues for consideration:

(1) What effect should the city council's action have on the report dated February 1, 1970, by Kline & Keith?

(2) What should be the auditor's responsibility for discovery and disclosure of events subsequent to the balance sheet date?

National Radiotronics, Inc.

National Radiotronics, Inc., is a large manufacturer and distributor of specialty parts and components for the electronics and electrical supply industries. Operating and financial difficulties became acute in 1970 thus presenting National's auditors with a reporting problem. Below are portions of the data from National's annual report:

	August 31	
	1970	1969
Receivables (Net)	$19,801,000	$18,870,000
Inventories (at FIFO, not exceeding market)	26,177,000	28,383,000
Fixed Assets (Net)	10,440,000	14,540,000
Total Assets	59,731,000	63,220,000
Notes Payable	21,807,000	23,774,000
Capital Stock	20,400,000	20,400,000
Retained Earnings (Deficit)	(3,146,000)	6,389,000

	12 Months Ended August 31	
	1970	1969
Net Sales:		
Specialty Parts and Components ...	$49,108,000	$48,644,000
Defense Group	13,230,000	22,280,000
Net Loss	9,535,000	1,887,000

In the spring of 1970, National's management decided to phase out its defense group and get out of government contracting. By July of 1970, all defense work had been completed or dropped and the company had disposed of nearly all of its equipment used in this segment of operations. Management was of the opinion that by dropping the defense group it could guide the company back into the "black." However, a special analysis by the company's independent auditors showed that the revenue from the specialty parts and components group failed to cover costs directly assignable to it by $1.1 million for the fiscal year 1970. The auditors found evidence of poor accounting control and serious lack of coordination in the company's purchasing, sales, and inventory policies in the specialty parts and components group.

Financial problems contributed to a worsening of National's headaches. Several bank and insurance company notes were in default and bills payable were not being met on a current basis. Creditors were demanding that additional security be provided and a clear threat of bankruptcy existed.

As a result of its financial woes, National received several offers for the purchase or merger of most of its operating divisions. As of October 31, 1970, the date of the auditor's report, management was giving serious consideration to the proposals of three companies.

The auditors felt that in the event of bankruptcy the loss might be as high as $6,300,000. On the other hand, if a sale or merger could be consummated with one of the interested companies, the ultimate loss would probably range between 10 to 20 percent of the stockholders' equity as of August 31, 1970. The auditors were of the opinion that bankruptcy could be avoided if a sale or merger was accomplished.

The auditor's report included the standard wording for the scope paragraph, which was followed by the middle paragraph shown below:

> The company experienced a loss of $9,535,000 for the year ended August 31, 1970. This loss includes a special charge of $1,320,000 resulting from the discontinuance and sale of all equipment of the government contracting division. Realization of the Company's inventories, receivables and property is dependent upon the successful future operations of the business. During 1970 the company has received and is considering several proposals for the purchase or merger of its specialty parts and components divisions. The loss, if any, from the sale or merger of the specialty parts and components divisions cannot be determined at the present time.

Issues for consideration:

(1) Suggest the appropriate wording for the opinion paragraph of the auditor's report.

(2) Would you change the wording if the company was not considering a sale or merger?

(3) Discuss the impact that uncertainty has on financial statements and on the auditor's opinion.

American Computronic Corp.

American Computronic Corp. is engaged in the design, development, and manufacture of specialized small computer systems, transmitting devices, and various peripheral computer equipment. It was formed in 1960 by three engineers who had extensive experience with a major computer manufacturer.

In 1968 American began an aggressive research and development (R&D) program to capture a large share of the fast-growing, specialized computer market. The aim of the program was a more active pursuit of the commercial customers. In the earlier years government sales had accounted for a major share of American's business. During 1968 and 1969 substantial costs were incurred for research and development; these costs were deferred and are being written off over a three-year period from January 1, 1970.

At December 31, 1970, the date of the audit examination by Estien & Lowe, CPA's, five specialized computer systems had been designed and developed. However, two of these showed little or no promise of marketability and the director of R&D confirmed that these had been abandoned. Of the remaining three systems, two have been marketed; however, the low volume of sales and initial production problems have resulted in a breakeven situation to date. Management is optimistic about the future of these two systems. The other system, while completely designed, has not been placed in production. The sales manager has high hopes for this model and sees it as the most profitable idea that R&D has come up with so far.

Since recovery of the research and development costs of $1,343,000 at December 31, 1970, was very uncertain, the auditors felt that these costs should be charged to expense in 1970. Management, on the other hand, believed that the research and development costs would be recovered in the future and issued a letter to this effect to the auditors. The production manager explained that production problems were now largely under control.

In their review, the auditors learned that forecasts made early in 1969 projected that average monthly deliveries by July of 1969 would be 20 systems per month. Delivery for all of 1970 totaled only 63 systems.

A summary of significant data from the financial statements appears below:

December 31, 1970

Current Assets	$4,259,000
Plant and Equipment (Net)	1,337,000
Deferred Research and Development Costs	1,893,000*
Other Assets	241,000
Total Assets	$7,730,000

Current Liabilities	$3,617,000
First Mortgage Note	1,410,000
Paid-In Capital	3,422,000
Retained Earnings (Deficit)	(719,000)
Total Equities	$7,730,000

12 Months Ended December 31, 1970

Sales	$4,839,000
Cost of Sales	$3,054,000
Selling, General, and Administrative Expense	2,388,000
Interest and Other Expense	136,000
	$5,578,000
Net Loss	$ 739,000

*$550,000 represent costs in developing peripheral equipment which appear fully recoverable.

The auditor's report contained a middle paragraph as follows:

The Company's balance sheet at December 31, 1970, includes $1,893,000 of deferred research and development costs which have been incurred in researching and developing new products for the commercial market. The realization of these costs is dependent upon the successful production and sales of the products at prices which will cover costs to produce and sell, including amortization of the deferred research and development costs.

The opinion paragraph commenced with the phrase, "Subject to the matter referred to in the above paragraph," and then continued with the standard wording of the opinion paragraph.

Issues for consideration:

(1) Comment on the position taken by the auditors with respect to the accounting for research and development costs. What other alternatives might have been taken and what would have been the effect of each on the auditor's report?

(2) Do you agree with the report given? If not, why not?

(3) Do research and development costs qualify as an asset according to generally accepted accounting principles? Comment.

(4) If the client were willing to accept the auditors' recommendations, would this have permitted them to issue an unqualified report? Comment.

CASE NO. 30

Kraft Development Corp.

Kraft Development Corp. was formed in 1968 to develop and sell approximately 6,300 acres of land located near St. Louis, Missouri. Although the development was several miles out of the city, the rapid growth of the metropolitan area and the completion of an interstate highway in the vicinity indicated that the undertaking should be a successful one.

In 1970, prior to making substantial development expenditures, Kraft had its tract of land appraised by members of the American Institute of Real Estate Appraisers. The appraisal showed the value of the land to be substantially in excess of the cost shown in the accounting records. Consequently, in October of 1970, the carrying value of the land was adjusted to the amount shown in the appraisal less the estimated federal income taxes attributable to the appraisal increase.

By the audit date, December 31, 1970, the company had an agreement to sell 1,000 lots to a builder at a profitable price; however, this represented only a small portion of the total acreage. Utilities have not been installed and the major portion of the development work remains to be done.

Success of the venture is dependent upon the sale of the homesites and the various commercial centers. The building promoter, who is now holding the agreement to purchase 1,000 lots, has received over 400 applications, with deposits, for the purchase of homes. By December 31, 1970, about 200 applications had resulted in executed sales contracts. According to the building promoter the rising interest costs and the increasing difficulty of securing adequate financing arrangements have resulted in a slower than anticipated rate of sales contracts.

Kraft's condensed balance sheet as of December 31, 1970, appears on the next page.

In preparing the report on Kraft, the auditors faced two problems in the presentation of land in the financial statements. First, the land was presented at an amount substantially above cost. Second, full realization of land and development costs through future sales was uncertain.

Kraft Development Corp.
Balance Sheet
December 31, 1970

Cash		$ 677,000
Land — Approximately 6,300 Acres, at Appraisal Value (Cost $7,376,000)	$15,000,000	
Less Estimated Federal Income Taxes that Would be Payable on Sale of Land at Appraisal Value	3,812,000	11,188,000
Land Development Costs		1,871,000
Other Assets		226,000
Total Assets		$13,962,000
Current Liabilities		$ 243,000
Mortgage Debt		9,407,000
Capital Stock, $10 Par Value		500,000
Appraisal Surplus on Land		3,812,000
Total Equities		$13,962,000

Issues for consideration:

(1) Consider what type of opinion you would recommend if the appraisal had not been recorded but the appraisal information had been shown in a note to the financial statements. Explain.

(2) Consider what type of opinion you would recommend if there were no realization problem. Explain.

(3) Draft the auditor's report required in the situation shown.

Superior Tools, Inc.

The auditing firm of Kelly & Monroe was engaged to audit the financial statements of Superior Tools, Inc., for the year ended March 31, 1970. The company has not had an independent audit of its statements prior to 1970.

The company consists of two major operating divisions, an aircraft parts division and a tool and die division. The tool and die division operated at a profit during the year ended March 31, 1970, and has been successful for many years. However, the aircraft parts division had a loss of approximately 1½ million dollars for the year.

The company's condensed financial statements showed the following:

March 31, 1970

Current Assets	$3,669,000
Current Liabilities	2,451,000
Working Capital	$1,218,000
Plant and Equipment, Net (Includes $2,700,000 Attributable to Aircraft Parts Division)	4,582,000
Long-Term Debt	1,337,000
Stockholders' Equity	4,463,000

12 Months Ended March 31, 1970

Sales	$9,129,000
Cost of Sales	$6,476,000
Selling and Administrative Expense	3,504,000
Net Loss	$ 851,000

During the current fiscal year Superior moved its small aircraft parts operations into a much larger facility acquired in March 1969, from a major aircraft manufacturer. Management explained that most of the machinery and equipment was old and required major repairs that were expensed as incurred. In addition, as a result of the need to triple the work force, many of the new employees were inexperienced.

In light of the heavy loss in the aircraft parts division, the auditors expressed concern about the prospects for future losses and the possibility of Superior having to abandon the operation of this division.

Mr. Stevens, the president of Superior, and other corporate officers were firm in their contention that the aircraft division would not be discontinued. They felt that the loss during the fiscal year 1970 was due to the start-up costs for a new operation. Extensive effort had gone into making the acquired facility operative and in organizing the production flows. The new employees had been given training and close supervision and they were now ready to assume normal job responsibilities. As Mr. Stevens explained, the sales volume had been deliberately held down and the expenses permitted to run up to facilitate the "tooling-up" of the aircraft parts division.

Sales orders received for fiscal 1971 substantially exceeded sales in 1970 and the president was confident that the division would be "in the black" in fiscal 1971.

The auditors, after studying the evidence and management observations, summarized their tentative conclusions in the following manner:

(1) Management will not dispose of the aircraft parts division.

(2) The forecast of operations for fiscal 1971 indicates that the problems responsible for the loss in 1970 will be corrected.

(3) The fiscal 1970 loss has resulted from start-up costs charged to the first year of operation of the acquired facility. Management might have altered the dimensions of the problem by deferring the costs incurred in placing the new facility in first-class working condition.

(4) Superior's management is effective and highly cost-conscious. Barring unusual obstacles, management has the capacity to guide operations to a profitable level.

Issues for consideration:

(1) What type of audit report would you issue on Superior's financial statements for fiscal 1970?

(2) Would you question the current charge-off of all the costs incurred in upgrading the facilities of the aircraft parts division and in training its new employees? Under the circumstances, do you agree that the income statement shows fairly the results of operations? Explain.

(3) What role should prospects for the future play in determining whether or not the current financial statements present fairly what they purport to present?

(4) What additional reporting issues does this case raise?

Nationwide Foods, Inc.

Nationwide Foods, Inc., was organized in 1968 to establish and franchise a national chain of food outlets. The outlets operate under the trade name of "Happy Kitchen" and were designed to be located along heavily traveled highways throughout the United States. The organizers of Nationwide expected to take advantage of the increasing tendency for Americans to travel by automobile for long distances. A national advertising campaign was planned to promote the new business.

Nationwide followed the procedure of building and furnishing the Happy Kitchen outlets and then selling the outlet to a local operator. The arrangement called for a small down payment (about 10%) and the execution of a 10-year note, secured by a mortgage on the property, for the balance of the price of the outlet. Each operator received training and supervision from Nationwide.

In October of 1970, Nationwide engaged the CPA firm of Antoine & Brenen to perform an audit for the year ended December 31, 1970. A summary of the data from the financial statements appears below and on the next page.

December 31, 1970

Current Assets	$ 459,000
Mortgage Notes Receivable From Franchises (Net of an Allowance of $138,000)	923,000
Other Assets	274,000
Total Assets	$1,656,000
Current Liabilities	$ 388,000
Long-Term Notes Payable	714,000
Capital Stock	400,000
Retained Earnings	154,000
Total Equities	$1,656,000

12 Months Ended December 31, 1970

Sales	$1,245,000
Costs and Expenses	1,108,000
Net Income	$ 137,000

At December 31, 1970, Nationwide had been in operation for only a short period but already had 50 "Happy Kitchens" in operation and seven were under construction. Although all of the outlets were considered to be potentially profitable, one half of them had been opened for less than one year.

Upon the advice of its auditors, Nationwide included an explanation of its operations and the nature of the receivables from its franchises in Note 1 to the financial statements. The note observed that the eventual collectibility of the long-term receivables was not readily determinable at the balance sheet date. The auditors considered the allowance for bad debts to be adequate based on the limited experience to date.

Issues for consideration:

(1) In the above instance, what type of opinion would you recommend? Explain fully.

(2) If Nationwide had been in existence for a period of ten years, what influence would this have on the auditors' opinion?

(3) Discuss the nature of the uncertainty posed in the above case. What impact does uncertainty have on the auditor's report?

Ramco, Inc.

Ramco, Inc., operates several steel fabricating plants in the Midwest. Although Ramco has been in operation for over 40 years, its earnings pattern in the last 10 years has become very erratic and the general financial position of the company has deteriorated.

The company's earnings history and financial position are summarized below: (Amounts in thousands of dollars)

	Sales	Net Earnings-Loss*	Dividends
1961	$20,245	$265	$118
1962	23,882	288	143
1963	19,495	124	94
1964	18,907	272	137
1965	15,388	89*	112
1966	19,455	49	74
1967	21,118	126*	—
1968	23,264	173*	—
1969	21,891	847*	—
1970	22,540	67	—

	December 31	
	1970	1969
Current Assets	$4,135	$3,847
Plant and Equipment (Net)	3,887	4,224
Other Assets	1,046	972
Total Assets	$9,068	$9,043
Current Liabilities	$3,551	$3,375
Other Liabilities	1,045	1,263
Stockholders' Equity	4,472	4,405
Total Equities	$9,068	$9,043

In conducting its examination of Ramco's financial statements for the year ended December 31, 1970, the auditing firm of Benson & Smith gave careful consideration to the company's financial difficulties. There was ample evidence that the company needed to secure additional working capital if the current level of operations was to be maintained. The management of the company is hopeful that a $1,000,000 ten-year loan can be negotiated by placing a lien on the plant and equipment.

Since its inception, the company has elected to be self-insured for risks under the workmen's compensation laws of the states in which it has operations. The company has followed the practice of providing in the accounts for all known claims under the workmen's compensation laws. Most of the claims arise from long range respiratory health problems inherent in the nature of the steel cutting and grinding processes. Discussions with insurance companies have indicated that if outside insurance coverage is obtained, the required initial payment would be $500,000 and annual premiums would be about $250,000. The charge to operations under the self-insured plan for 1970 was $185,000 and claims over the past several years have been increasing.

The state workmen's compensation authorities have questioned the continued acceptability of the company's self-insured plan. After a series of meetings with the state authorities during December 1970, management received permission to continue, temporarily, its self-insured plan provided that immediate steps are taken to obtain outside insurance.

The company's financial statements for 1970 included a footnote explaining the self-insured plan and the conditions which the state workmen's compensation authorities have imposed on the company.

Ramco's management is very concerned about the wording of the auditors' report on the 1970 financial statements. The company's ability to borrow needed funds will be influenced in part by the nature of the audit report.

Issues for consideration:

(1) What wording would you suggest for the audit report that Benson & Smith should issue on the financial statements as of December 31, 1970?

(2) What adjustments to the financial statements would you recommend in order to cause the financial statements to present *more* fairly financial position and results of operations?

Chapter 3
Special
Reports

Statement No. 33 refers to special reports as those for which the wording of the usual short-form report may be inappropriate and for which special wording must be used in the opinion section. Such special reports may include (1) reports on financial statements of organizations utilizing a cash or other incomplete basis of accounting, (2) reports on financial statements of certain non-profit organizations utilizing accounting practices which differ from practices followed by profit-seeking business enterprises, and (3) reports prepared for limited purposes.

Generally accepted auditing standards are applicable to special reports. However, the first standard of reporting would not apply to special reports that do not seek to present financial position and results of operations. Correspondingly, the second, or consistency, standard of reporting would be applicable only in those instances where special reports are designed to show financial position and results of operations. The third and fourth reporting standards are applicable to special reports. Examples of various instances in which special reports may be applicable are as follows:

Financial statements of —

  Cash basis enterprises organized for profit (proprietorships, partnerships, and joint ventures)

  Certain non-profit organizations which follow accounting practices differing in some respects from those followed by enterprises organized for profit (governmental authorities and educational, religious and charitable institutions)

  Estates and trusts

  Certain regulated industries (life insurance companies)

  Companies in the development stage

  Companies in process of liquidation

Limited purpose reports —

    Compliance with certain provisions of bond indentures (compliance letters)

    Letters for underwriters (comfort letters)

    Computations of rentals, royalties, profit-sharing bonuses, price for sale of business, number of shares outstanding, and the like

    Purchase investigations

    Data prepared for filing with governmental authorities

    Status of income tax liability

    Forecasts

    Review of accounting procedures and internal controls.

The five cases in this chapter illustrate certain types of special reports. The first three cases deal with limited purpose reports (a compliance letter, a comfort letter, and a letter on a review of accounting procedures and internal control). The final two cases treat the reporting problem for organizations that follow accounting practices which differ in some respects with practices commonly followed by business enterprises organized for profit (a life insurance company and a trust).

Seanac Finance Corp.

Seanac Finance Corp., a wholly-owned subsidiary of National Auto Supplier, Inc., was organized to provide financing to National Auto's customers. National Auto franchises auto supply retail centers to customers owning an appropriate building and parking lot. Seanac's original capital structure was as follows:

6¼% Collateral Trust Notes	$3,500,000
5% Subordinated Debentures (Payable to National Auto)	2,000,000
Common Stock	500,000
	$6,000,000

Under the terms of the collateral trust indenture, Seanac's independent auditors were required to render a written statement that while examining Seanac's financial statements, they did not find any evidence of default by Seanac in fulfilling the provisions of the indenture. If an event of default were noted, the auditors were required to disclose the nature of it. The indenture sought to assure the holder of the collateral notes that Seanac's resources are invested in eligible real estate loans. Eligible loans are defined as those which are not more than 90 days past due. Seanac's net worth plus the subordinated debentures must, at all times, be maintained at an amount in excess of 60% of the collateral notes. Net worth was defined as the net worth shown by the financial statement less the amount of any ineligible loans.

At September 30, 1970, the closing date of Seanac's fiscal year, the auditors' examination revealed that Seanac was in violation of the 60% requirement as provided for in the indenture. In November 1970, National Auto purchased for cash an "ineligible" mortgage loan in the amount of $300,000 from Seanac. As a result the event of default existing at September 30 was removed. The event of default and subsequent remedy thereof were mentioned in the notes to the financial statements, but the auditor's report dated December 2, 1970, did not contain any qualifications.

Issues for consideration:

(1) Prepare the compliance letter which the collateral trust indenture calls for. The letter should be dated December 2, 1970.

(2) If the event of default had not been removed by December 2, 1970, what effect would this have had on (a) the auditor's report, and (b) the compliance letter?

Beef Burgers, Inc.

Carolina Tobacco Corp., a large tobacco company interested in diversification, entered into an agreement to purchase 95% or more of the outstanding stock (1,972,000 shares) of Beef Burgers, Inc. The purchase price was $11 per share and the closing date of the agreement was June 12, 1970. The price was arrived at by applying a factor of 20 to the earnings per share shown by Beef Burgers' financial statements for the fiscal year ended January 31, 1970.

Beef Burgers owned a chain of sandwich outlets operating in 16 states. The latest audited financial statements of Beef Burgers were for the year ended January 31, 1970. As part of the purchase agreement, Carolina Tobacco requested that Beef Burgers' auditors, Riner & Wicksen, issue a comfort letter covering the period from January 31, 1970, to June 7, 1970. The comfort letter was to disclose any material adverse changes in financial position and results of operations during the specified period.

Beef Burgers routinely prepared monthly financial statements and the auditors reviewed these statements for the four months ended May 31, 1970. These statements were compared with the corresponding statements for 1969, revealing the following changes:

| | Four Months Ended May 31 | | | |
	1970		1969	
Sales	$3,354,000	100.0%	$3,102,000	100.0%
Gross Profit	1,191,000	35.5%	1,148,000	37.0%
Income from Operations	737,900	22.0%	732,100	23.6%

The auditors' inquiries revealed that the major factor in the reduction in the gross profit percentage was an increase in the cost of the food and paper used in the sandwich operations. The auditors also read the minutes of all meetings of the Board of Directors and the Executive Committee from February 1 through June 7, 1970, and discussed the operations of the company with the controller and the secretary-treasurer. The company officials, including the president, assured the auditors that there had not been any material adverse change in the company's operations. The auditors did not observe anything which caused them to disbelieve the officers.

Issues for consideration:

(1) Draft the comfort letter that the auditors should issue. Should the percentage change in gross profit and operating income be disclosed? What else should be disclosed in the letter? What limitations should be clearly set forth in the letter?

(2) Discuss the phrase "nothing came to our attention which would cause us to believe that. . . . " Comment on the degree of responsibility the auditor assumes as a result of making this statement.

Friendly Finance Company

Friendly Finance Company was organized as a consumer finance company in 1955 by L. P. Grady and Alan Young of St. Louis, Missouri. The company expanded very rapidly, and by 1970 consisted of 27 consumer finance offices in the St. Louis area with outstanding loan balances of $17 million.

As part of its financing program, Friendly Finance established a line of credit with one of St. Louis' largest banks. By January 1970, this "line" to Friendly Finance had increased to $5 million.

During the spring of 1970, Friendly Finance experienced a "profit squeeze" due to increased interest rates and higher bad debt losses resulting from a downturn in business conditions. Friendly Finance also encountered problems in maintaining effective operating control over the various loan offices. In early 1969 a new accounting system, utilizing a computer, had been installed at the central administrative offices of Friendly Finance to economize the servicing of loans and to help improve the internal control over the loan offices. The data processing department encountered many problems in making the change over to the new system; these problems continued into 1970.

In June 1970 a suburban loan office of Friendly Finance was forced to close as a result of the misappropriation of funds by four employees of that office, including the assistant manager. When the St. Louis bank that had been furnishing Friendly Finance's line of credit learned of the weaknesses in the Company's internal control system, it demanded that the management of Friendly Finance take immediate steps to improve financial and operating controls throughout the company. The bank further stipulated that a firm of certified public accountants, agreeable to both the bank and Friendly Finance, be engaged to evaluate thoroughly and report on the adequacy of Friendly Finance's internal control system.

The CPA firm of Burley & Cox was appointed in July to conduct the special study and was directed to present its findings and conclusions to a joint meeting of two bank vice-presidents and the top administrative officers of Friendly Finance. The report of Burley & Cox was scheduled to be presented on October 1, 1970.

Burley & Cox conducted its examination of the company's internal control system and its operation during August and September. The examination showed that the corrective steps taken by the company during June and July provided it with an adequate and effective system of control procedures. The CPA firm realized, however, that the successful operation of the improved control system depended upon careful and continuous surveillance by the management of the company.

Issues for consideration:

(1) What special reporting problem does the auditor face when asked to evaluate and report on the "adequacy" of a client's internal control system?

(2) In the circumstances described above, what wording would you recommend that the auditors use in their report to the company and the bank?

Southeastern Insurance Company

Southeastern Insurance Company is a life insurance company domiciled in South Carolina and doing business throughout the southeastern part of the United States. Southeastern was organized in 1946 and at December 31, 1970, had insurance in force of $450,000,000. The company has approximately 450 stockholders. Pertinent data from Southeastern's December 31, 1970, financial statements are as follows:

December 31, 1970

Investments	$18,500,000
Accrued Premiums and Other Assets	2,100,000
	$20,600,000
Life Policy Reserves	$12,500,000
Other Liabilities	2,500,000
Stockholders' Equity	5,600,000
	$20,600,000

12 Months Ended December 31, 1970

Life Insurance Premiums	$ 5,100,000
Investment Income	900,000
	$ 6,000,000
Costs and Expenses	5,800,000
Net Income	$ 200,000

Until 1970 the company's financial statements had not been audited. However, as a result of a slowdown in the amount of life insurance put on the books in 1969 and 1970, certain groups of stockholders had pressed for more financial information, including audited financial statements. Thus, in January 1971, the president of Southeastern contacted the auditing firm of Lambert, Magee & Rone to make an examination of the company's financial statements for the year ended December 31, 1970.

At the end of the examination, the auditors found that they had a significant reporting problem because the financial statements of Southeastern, under the laws of the State of South Carolina, were required to be prepared on the basis of regulations published by the insurance commission of South Carolina. Certain of the accounting practices prescribed by the insurance commission vary significantly from generally accepted accounting principles employed in other industries. The following note to Southeastern's financial statements described these variances:

The accompanying financial statements have been prepared in conformity with accounting practices prescribed or permitted by insurance regulatory authorities. Such practices differ from those generally accepted accounting principles commonly followed by other types of enterprises in that (a) certain assets designated as "nonadmitted assets" are excluded from the balance sheet and are charged directly to unassigned surplus, and (b) commissions and other costs of acquiring new business are charged to expense as incurred rather than being amortized over the expected terms of the policies; however, certain life policy reserves are provided on a modified preliminary term method which requires smaller first-year provisions and tends to offset the cost of writing new business. The aggregate net effect of such variations on the financial statements has not been determined; however, management estimates that such variations have reduced net income and unassigned surplus.

The nonadmitted assets which have been excluded from the accompanying balance sheet consist of the following items:

Agents' balances	$422,000
Furniture and Equipment	124,000
	$546,000

The effect on the financial statements of item (b) above was not available and the company did not choose to accurately determine the effect because of the prohibitive cost of making the calculations for each of the thousands of policies in force. Rough estimates by the company indicated that these practices had resulted in a material understatement of net income in recent years and a material understatement of stockholders' equity at December 31, 1970, when compared to generally accepted accounting principles employed in other industries.

Issues for consideration:

(1) What type of report should the auditors issue on the financial statements as of December 31, 1970?

(2) If certain well-defined procedures (or practices) are applied universally in the financial statements of an industry, do these procedures or practices qualify as "generally accepted" as that term is generally understood?

(3) Discuss the soundness of the accounting practices employed in the insurance industry.

The Baker Trust

Mr. Renwick T. Baker, who died March 20, 1969, established a testamentary trust for the benefit of his wife and three sons. The trust property originally consisted of residential and commercial real estate in Tulsa, Oklahoma, and included undeveloped lands outside the city limits. The trust instrument provided that the income of the trust, as defined, was to be distributed to Mrs. Baker on a current basis during her lifetime and that upon her death, the principal was to be transferred to the three sons. The trustee was instructed to distribute to Mrs. Baker, on a quarterly basis, the excess of the total income from the property over expenses (which includes necessary maintenance of the properties and a provision for depreciation on only the commercial properties). The trustee invested the undistributed income represented by the depreciation on the commercial properties.

Below is a summary of the assets and liabilities of the trust as of December 31, 1970:

Cash	$ 14,100
Savings Certificates	17,600
Residential Real Estate	143,000
Commercial Real Estate	
(Net of depreciation)	289,400
Unimproved Property	244,000
	$708,100
Payable to Trustee	$ 4,300
Undistributed Income	9,800
Trust Principal	694,000
	$708,100

The trust's income for the 12 months ended December 31, 1970, was $49,200; its expenses, including depreciation, totaled $16,100.

In the audit of The Baker Trust, Van Rees & Merrick, CPA's, learned that the trust's financial statements were prepared on the cash basis of accounting as required by the trust instrument. The unrecorded interest and rentals amounted to less than 5% of the total assets of the trust at December 31, 1970. Net income for the year on the cash basis was not materially different from that on the accrual basis.

Issues for consideration:

(1) Should Van Rees & Merrick issue a standard short-form report on The Baker Trust? If not, suggest the appropriate wording of the auditor's report.

(2) What changes would you make in the auditor's report if the difference between the cash and accrual basis was material?

Chapter 4

The Auditor's Legal Responsibilities

The auditor has a responsibility to management, creditors, stockholders, and others to perform his work according to the standards set by his profession. As a member of a profession the auditor has a legal liability to those who use and rely on his reports under common law and statutes. The extent of the auditor's liability has expanded over the years. Recent developments in the area of the auditor's legal liability have been most significant and have raised some fundamental and crucial issues.

In this chapter, the auditor's liability to clients, third parties, and under Federal Securities statutes is summarized. The key issues raised by recent court developments are set forth for consideration. Finally, three recent landmark type cases are reviewed. These cases may well result in a material stretching of the boundary of legal liability of the auditor. The three cases are included, with reproduction of key portions of testimony, to aid the reader in appreciating the grave importance of the auditor's using "due professional care" in all of his work and particularly in the preparation of audit reports.

Liability to Clients

The auditor's liability to his client has generally been limited to failure to exercise due professional care in the performance of a contract, usually the examination of the client's financial statements. The auditor can usually be held liable to his client for ordinary negligence in the performance of his duties. The performance to which the auditor is held includes specific contractual provisions, such as conducting his examination in accordance with generally accepted auditing standards and the preparation and filing of income tax returns in accordance with applicable rules and regulations.

It is also generally believed that when a specified non-client relies on the auditor's report and the auditor either had or should have had knowledge of such reliance, the auditor will be liable for ordinary negligence.

Liability to Third Parties

Legal action by third party users who are members of a general class has generally been limited to those situations where the auditor has been shown to be guilty of fraud or *gross* negligence. This basic doctrine was enunciated in the Ultramares decision (Ultramares Corp. v. Touche, 255 N.Y. 170) written by Justice Cordozo in 1931. The Ultramares decision defines fraud to include a "pretense of knowledge" when there is in fact no knowledge. Since the 1930's, auditors have been operating under the general rule that liability to third parties is restricted to instances where gross negligence or constructive fraud is evident.

Liability under Federal Securities Statutes

The auditor's liability to users of financial statements was materially extended by the Federal Securities Act of 1933 and the Securities Exchange Act of 1934. The Securities Act of 1933 exposes the auditor to claims for damage by users for false or misleading statements or misleading omissions in the financial statements. Thus, the auditor may be held guilty for negligence or fraud and the plaintiff need not prove reliance on the financial statements. Further, the defendant must assume the burden of showing that after a reasonable examination he had reasonable grounds to believe and did believe that the financial statements were true and reliable. The Securities Exchange Act of 1934 imposes upon the plaintiff the duty to show reliance and to establish that such reliance was in fact the primary cause of his losses. In addition, the 1934 Act permits the auditor the defense that "he acted in good faith and has no knowledge that such statement was false or misleading." It appears that the 1934 Act does not open the door to liability for ordinary negligence on the part of the auditor.

Issues Raised by Recent Court Developments

The decade of the 1960's has ushered in some unprecedented developments in the area of the auditor's legal responsibilities. Recent court cases involving the nature and extent of legal liability are of critical importance to every auditor and when finally resolved they will probably represent new precedents.

Several fundamental and vexing issues emerge in the recent significant court cases reviewed in this chapter. Some of these are included here as an introduction and encouragement to the reader to probe the materials carefully.

As previously noted, the Ultramares decision refrained from extending liability on the part of the auditor to an indeterminate class of third party users for ordinary negligence. Part of the rationale of the

Ultramares decision seems to be based, in part at least, on the notion that, although the auditor was aware that the financial statements were to be distributed to creditors, the financial statements were for the "primary benefit" of the client. It is not difficult to speculate that as the audit function becomes recognized basically as an attestation for the benefit of third party users, the auditor's legal responsibility to perform his duties without negligence will extend to these users of financial statements.

Closely related to the "benefit rule" doctrine is the matter of the auditor's independence and its importance. If the role of the auditor is that of impartial reviewer of management's (client) financial statements in order to lend credence to such statements by third party users, then independence is vital in the auditor's relationship to management. It follows that the courts may be increasingly critical in their scrutiny of the auditor's relationship to management.

The auditing profession has long held, with seeming propriety, that the fairest test of an auditor's conduct is to compare his actions with those which would have been taken by another competent auditor applying the standards of the profession in similar circumstances. The critical issue here is whether a person should be held guilty for shortcomings of his profession's standards of practice. In other words, should an auditor be held legally liable if he has performed an audit in accordance with generally accepted auditing standards? When the issue is seen as the standards of a professional group vis-a-vis the expectations of society, it is clear that the larger group must prevail. It seems, however, that the courts should weigh carefully the standards of a profession in judging one of its members and the evidence should be overwhelming before a member is held guilty for conduct which a respected profession prescribes.

Perhaps one of the most ominous developments in recent court cases is that of charging the auditor with criminal conspiracy in the issuance of financial statements. This presents new hazards to a professional auditor in his practice and may be a sign of significant changes in auditing practices to minimize this additional exposure.

Review of Court Cases

The following cases are intended to be representative of some of the significant legal cases which have been considered recently by the courts. The opinions cited are in the exact words of the source, although the text may be cut for the sake of brevity. Any omissions in the text are noted by * * *.

The Yale Express System, Inc. Case

The Yale Express System, Inc., case is a class action brought against an auditing firm under the Securities Exchange Act and common law deceit doctrines. The plaintiffs contended that the auditors, after learning that financial statements of Yale Express, upon which they had previously reported, were false and misleading, failed to disclose such findings on a timely basis; as a result, the plaintiffs asserted that the auditors were liable for damages. Knowledge of the falsity of the financial statements was obtained by the auditing firm while conducting a management services engagement for Yale Express. The auditors were also charged with failure to disclose that unaudited interim financial statements issued by Yale Express contained inaccuracies.

Reproduced below are parts of the opinion of a United States District Court judge denying a motion by the defendant auditing firm for a dismissal of certain of the charges against it.

Fischer v. Kletz
266 F. Supp. 180 (S.D.N.Y. 1967)

Action against accounting firm for damages in connection with corporation's financial statement, which accountants had certified, and interim statements issued by corporation. Defendants cross moved to dismiss. The District Court, Tyler, J., held, inter alia, that complaint against accountants for failure to disclose after-acquired information that statement was false was sufficient, as against motion to dismiss, under Securities Exchange Act provision relating to manipulative and deceptive devices, although accountants did not gain from nondisclosure, despite lack of privity between plaintiffs and accountants, and despite lack of specific assertion that accountants had aided and abetted corporation in publishing statement. Motion denied.

* * *

TYLER, D. J. ... In October, 1966, plaintiffs in this class action[1] moved against defendant Peat, Marwick, Mitchell & Co. ("PMM") for further discovery under Rule 34, F.R.Civ.P., based in part upon the allegations set forth in paragraphs 25 through 25.3 of the second consolidated amended complaint (hereinafter "the complaint"). PMM

---

[1] For other published opinions dealing with this controversy, see D.C., 249 F.Supp. 539 (Jan. 13, 1966) (denial of motion to dismiss or, in alternative, for stay pending resolution of certain factual determinations by ICC) and D.C., 41 F.R.D. 377 (Dec. 8, 1966) (determination that a class action can be maintained).

opposed this motion, and, in addition, cross-moved against the plaintiffs, pursuant to Rule 12(b) (1) and/or 12(b) (6), F.R.Civ.P., for an order by this court dismissing paragraphs 25–25.3 of the complaint on the grounds that the court has no jurisdiction over the subject matter contained therein and/or that the allegations of these paragraphs fail to state a claim upon which relief can be granted. Plaintiffs and the Securities and Exchange Commission ("SEC"), which has filed an *amicus curiae* brief, strenuously oppose the cross-motion.

The discovery motion was disposed of by this court in a memorandum opinion, dated November 1, 1966; this opinion will deal with PMM's cross-motion to dismiss paragraphs 25–25.3 of the complaint.

For the purposes of this motion, the parties agree in principle that the facts urged upon the court by the plaintiffs must be accepted as true and that the challenged portions of the complaint must be upheld if they are supported by any viable rule of law. There follows a summarization of the facts which reasonably can be read from the formal complaint allegations, particularly those under fire in this motion.

Sometime early in 1964, PMM, acting as an independent public accountant, undertook the job of auditing the financial statements that Yale Express System, Inc. ("Yale"), a national transportation concern, intended to include in the annual report to its stockholders for the year ending December 31, 1963. On March 31, 1964, PMM certified the figures contained in these statements. On or about April 9, the annual report containing the certification was issued to the stockholders of Yale. Subsequently, on or about June 29, 1964, a Form 10–K Report, containing the same financial statements as the annual report, was filed with the SEC as required by that agency's rules and regulations.

At an unspecified date "early in 1964," probably shortly after the completion of the audit, Yale engaged PMM to conduct so-called "special studies" of Yale's past and current income and expenses. In the course of this special assignment, sometime presumably before the end of 1964,[2] PMM discovered that the figures in the annual report were substantially false and misleading.

---

[2]There is a factual dispute here. PMM maintains that the falsity of the figures was discovered after the filing of the required 10–K report with the SEC on June 29, 1964; plaintiffs contend that the discovery was made before this filing.

Not until May 5, 1965, however, when the results of the special studies were released, did PMM disclose this finding to the exchanges on which Yale securities were traded, to the SEC or to the public at large.

Furthermore, during the course of PMM's special studies, Yale periodically announced to PMM an intention to issue several interim statements and reports to show the company's 1964 financial performance. In at least two instances, Yale was told by PMM that figures derived from the special studies could not be used as a basis for these interim statements; in addition, PMM recommended that the figures developed by Yale through its internal accounting procedures be used in the reports.

Yale thereupon issued several interim statements containing figures which were not compiled, audited or certified by PMM. As in the case of the annual and SEC reports, later developments revealed that the figures contained in these interim statements were materially false and misleading.

Plaintiffs allege that, from the compilation of figures for 1964 and its knowledge of the contents of the interim reports, PMM knew that the figures contained in those statements were grossly inaccurate. No disclosure of this finding has yet been made to the exchanges, the SEC or the public.

Within this alleged factual context, the plaintiffs assert that PMM is liable in damages for its failure to disclose not only that the certified financial statements in the 1963 annual report contained false and misleading figures but also that the interim statements issued by Yale were inaccurate. Because the bases for such claimed liability are grounded on distinctly different legal theories, the issues unique to each area will be discussed and analyzed separately.

I.

Annual Report Liability

Plaintiffs attack PMM for its silence and inaction after its employees discovered, during the special studies, that the audited and certified figures in the financial statements reflecting Yale's 1963 performance were grossly inaccurate. They contend that inasmuch as PMM knew that its audit and certificate would be relied upon by the investing public,[3] the accounting firm had a duty to alert the public in some way that the audited and certified statements were materially false and inaccurate. PMM counters that there is no common law or statutory basis for imposing such a duty on it as a public accounting firm retained by the officers and directors of Yale.

Strict analysis leads to the conclusion that PMM is attacked in the complaint because it wore two hats in conducting its business relations with Yale during the period in question. PMM audited and certified the financial statements in the 1963 annual report and Form 10-K as a statutory "independent public accountant"[4] whose responsibility

is not only to the client who pays his fee, but also to investors, creditors and others who may rely on the financial statements which he certifies.   *   *   *

The public accountant must report fairly on the facts as he finds them whether favorable or unfavorable to his client. His duty is to safeguard the public interest, not that of his client. (In the Matter of Touche, Niven, Bailey & Smart, 37 S.E.C. 629, 670-671 (1957)) (footnotes omitted)

Following the certification, PMM switched its role to that of an accountant employed by Yale to undertake special studies which were necessitated by business demands rather than by statutory or regulatory requirements. In this sense, it can be seen that during the special studies PMM was a "dependent public accountant" whose primary obligations, under normal circumstances, were to its client and not the public.

It was, of course, during the conduct of the special studies that the inaccuracies in the audited and certified statements were discovered. The time of this discovery makes the questions here involved difficult and unique. On the basis of the Commission's *Touche, Niven* opinion,

[3] The several issues involving reliance can be finally resolved only when the facts are more fully, if not completely, developed.

[4] Since Yale's securities were registered on the New York Stock Exchange, Yale was required to have its annual report certified by an "independent public accountant." Section 13(a) (2) of the Securities Exchange Act of 1934, 15 U.S.C. § 78m (a) (2).

an accountant has a duty to the investing public to certify only those statements which he deems accurate. This duty is not directly involved here, however, for the inaccuracies were discovered after the certification had been made and the 1963 annual report had been released. PMM maintains, therefore, that any duty to the investing public terminated once it certified the relevant financial statements. Plaintiffs, of course, contend to the contrary. Thus, the serious question arises as to whether or not an obligation correlative to but conceptually different from the duty to audit and to certify with reasonable care and professional competence[5] arose as a result of the circumstance that PMM knew that investors were relying upon its certification of the financial statements in Yale's annual report.

A. Common Law Liability

Plaintiffs' claim is grounded in the common law action of deceit, albeit an unusual type in that most cases of deceit involve an affirmative misrepresentation by the defendant.[6] Here, however, plaintiffs attack PMM's nondisclosure or silence.

* * *

Generally speaking, I can see no reason why this duty to disclose should not be imposed upon an accounting firm which makes a representation it knows will be relied upon by investors. To be sure, certification of a financial statement does not create a formal business relationship between the accountant who certifies and the individual who relies upon the certificate for investment purposes. The act of certification, however, is similar in its effect to a representation made in a business transaction: both supply information which is naturally and justifiably relied upon by individuals for decisional purposes.

---

[5]Breach of this duty is alleged in paragraph 26.1 of the second consolidated amended complaint but, of course, is not in issue here.

[6]The complaint allegations attacked on this motion which are based on common law principles are subject to the pendent jurisdiction of this court. Although the parties are silent on the point, I have assumed that under the circumstances suggested by the complaint as a whole, this court should look to New York law on the questions here presented. No New York cases particularly in point have been found; however, it seems fair to assume that the New York courts would look to and apply the principles of the authorities herein discussed.

Viewed in this context of the impact of nondisclosure on the injured party, it is difficult to conceive that a distinction between accountants and parties to a business transaction is warranted. The elements of "good faith and common honesty" which govern the businessman presumably should also apply to the statutory "independent public accountant."

PMM, of course, disputes the imposition of a duty to disclose and, for its purposes, properly emphasizes that the Restatement speaks in terms of "a business transaction" to which the alleged tort-feasor is a party and in which he has a definite pecuniary interest. Indeed, the cases discussed and cited heretofore involve instances where both plaintiff and defendant are economically affected by the defendant's nondisclosure.

PMM contends that the duty imposed on a party to a business transaction to disclose that a prior representation is false and misleading is "in no way pertinent to the standard of responsibility applicable to the independent auditor" (PMM's Reply Brief, p. 8) and that the obligation to disclose is contingent upon the presence of the opportunity for the accrual of personal gain to the nondisclosure party as a result of the nondisclosure.

The parties and the SEC have not supplied, nor has the court found, any cases which analyze the issue raised by this contention within a factual framework involving nondisclosure of information which makes a prior representation false. As the ensuing discussion will show, however, this does not mean that plaintiffs' cause of action for deceit must be dismissed at this stage of this litigation, nor does it preclude a rational analysis of the issue raised by defendant.

In cases involving affirmative misrepresentations, it is now the settled rule that a misrepresenter can be held liable, regardless of his interest in the transaction.

* * *

In my view, accepting the pertinent allegations of the complaint to be true, PMM must be regarded as bound at this preliminary stage of the litigation by this rule of law. Though concededly "disinterested" in the sense that it achieved no advantage by its silence, PMM is charged in the complaint for losses realized by plaintiffs as a result of its nondisclosure. This is sufficient, at least in the pleading sense, under the cases discussed, save for one remaining problem — whether or not plaintiffs must plead and ultimately prove intent by PMM to deceive by its silence.

In Endsley v. Johns, supra, and James-Dickinson Farm Mortgage Co. v. Harry, supra, the court in each case, it is true, suggested that one of the elements necessary to support the cause of action was an intention by defendant to deceive plaintiff. In the present case involving nondisclosure of information which makes false a prior representation on which plaintiffs claimed to have justifiably relied, it can be argued that, absent proper allegations of intent to deceive, PMM is entitled to dismissal.

Careful reflection upon the ramifications of the basic rules of deceit liability constrain me to reject this argument, pending full resolution of the facts of this case.

Liability in a case of nondisclosure is based upon the breach of a duty imposed by the demands of "good faith and common honesty." Loewer v. Harris, 57 F. at 373. The imposition of the duty creates an objective standard against which to measure a defendant's actions and leaves no room for an analysis of the subjective considerations inherent in the area of intent. Thus, to base liability in part upon subjective standards of intent of the nondisclosing defendant would blur and weaken the objective basis of impact of nondisclosure upon the plaintiff. In the alternative, if this rationale be deemed unacceptable, it can be persuasively urged that in a nondisclosure case, intent can be sensibly imputed to a defendant who, knowing that plaintiff will rely upon his original representations, sits by silently when they turn out to be false.

In light of the foregoing discussion, I find no sound reasons to justify barring plaintiffs from the opportunity to prove a common-law action of deceit against PMM. It is true that each case cited and discussed above is factually distinguishable from the case at bar. But the distinctions create no presently discernible, substantial differences of law or policy. The common law has long required that a person who has made a representation must correct that representation if it becomes false and if he knows people are relying on it. This duty to disclose is imposed regardless of the interest of defendant in the representation and subsequent nondisclosure. Plaintiffs have sufficiently alleged the elements of nondisclosure on the part of this "disinterested" defendant. Accordingly, they must be given an opportunity to prove those allegations.

To conclude thus is not to ignore the manifold difficulties that a final determination of liability on the part of public accountants for nondisclosure would create for professional firms and other business entities (and, indeed, individuals) similarly situated. Some obvious questions can be briefly set forth as examples of such potential problems. How long, for instance, does the duty to disclose after-acquired information last? To whom and how should disclosure be made? Does liability exist if the after-acquired knowledge is obtained from a source other than the original supplier of information? Is there a duty to disclose if an associate or employee of the accounting firm discovers that the financial statements are false but fails to report it to the firm members?

These and similar questions briefly indicate the potentially significant impact upon accountants, lawyers and business entities in the event that a precise rule or rules of liability for nondisclosure are fashioned and recognized in the law. On the other side of the coin, however, as the bulk of the discussion hereinbefore has shown, investors in publicly-held companies have a strong interest in being afforded some degree of protection by and from those professional and business persons whose representations are relied upon for decisional purposes. In my view, resolution of the issues posed by the complaint allegations here in question must be made with these important but conflicting interests in mind. Proper reconciliation of these interests or policy considerations, however, can only be made after full development of the facts of this case during the discovery process and at trial.

B. Section 18 Liability

Section 18(a) of the Securities Exchange Act of 1934[7] specifically imposes civil liability upon

> any person who shall make or cause to be made any statement in any * * * report * * * filed pursuant to this title or any rule or regulation thereunder * * *, which statement was at the time and in the light of the circumstances under which it was made false or misleading with respect to any material fact * * *

It is uncontroverted that, on June 29, 1964, Yale filed with the SEC a 10–K Report, which contained, *inter alia,* PMM's certificate of the corporation's financial statements. Plaintiffs contend that PMM knew before the date of filing that the financial statements were false and submit that by allowing the statements to be filed, defendant "in effect caused a false certificate to be filed with the SEC. Liability would necessarily follow under § 18." (Plaintiffs' Memorandum, p. 21).

Denying liability generally under Section 18, PMM specifically denies the allegation that it had discovered the falsity of the figures prior to or at the time of filing. It is thus obvious that a serious factual dispute is present here.[8] In light of this, I deem it advisable to defer resolution of the issue of PMM's Section 18 liability until the facts are more fully developed.

Accordingly, that portion of the motion to dismiss addressed to Section 18 of the 1934 Act is denied without prejudice to renewal at trial.

C. Section 10(b) and Rule 10b-5 Liability

Plaintiffs additionally argue that the disputed allegations against PMM can be maintained under Section 10(b) of the Securities Ex-

[7]15 U.S.C. § 78r.

[8]Robert G. Conroy, a partner of PMM, has submitted an affidavit in which, after discussing PMM's total lack of connection with the filing of the 10–K Report, he states, "In any event, PMM did not discover discrepancies in the 1963 financial statements on which PMM had rendered an opinion until well after the June 29, 1964 filing date." Plaintiffs contend PMM's "discovery of management's alleged deception [was] well in advance" of the filing of the 10–K Report (Plaintiff's Memorandum, p. 19).

change Act[9] and SEC Rule 10b–5,[10] promulgated thereunder.[11] PMM contends to the contrary and moves to dismiss any part of paragraphs 25–25.3 of the operative complaint which is grounded upon Section 10(b) and Rule 10b–5. Resolution of the issue created by these conflicting contentions is complicated by a comparison of the status of PMM with that of other defendants in reported cases dealing with civil liability under Section 10(b) and Rule 10b–5.

It is now axiomatic that a private remedy exists for defrauded investors under Section 10(b) and Rule 10b–5. See 3 Loss, Securities Regulation 1763 (1961 ed.). Moreover, the statute and rule both state that they may be invoked against "any person" who indulges in fraudulent practices in connection with the purchase or sale of securities. In actual practice, however, defendants in Section 10(b) and Rule 10b–5 cases have tended to fall into four general categories. The first three are (1) insiders, (2) broker–dealers, and (3) corporations whose stock is purchased or sold by plaintiffs. Common to each of these categories is the possibility that economic gain or advantage will result from the fraudulent practices alleged in the complaint. The fourth

---

[9] 15 U.S.C. § 78j(b). The subsection provides as follows:
"It shall be unlawful for any person, directly or indirectly, by the use of any means or instrumentality of interstate commerce or of the mails, or of any facility of any national securities exchange —

* * * * * *

(b) To use or employ, in connection with the purchase or sale of any security registered on a national securities exchange or any security not so registered, any manipulative or deceptive device or contrivance in contravention of such rules and regulations as the Commission may prescribe as necessary or appropriate in the public interest or for the protection of investors."

[10] 17 C.F.R. § 240.10b–5 (hereinafter Rule 10b–5). The rule provides as follows:
"It shall be unlawful for any person, directly or indirectly, by the use of any means or instrumentality of interstate commerce, or of the mails, or of any facility of any national securities exchange,
(a) To employ any device, scheme, or artifice to defraud,
(b) To make any untrue statement of a material fact or to omit to state a material fact necessary in order to make the statements made, in the light of the circumstances under which they were made, not misleading, or
(c) To engage in any act, practice, or course of business which operates or would operate as a fraud or deceit upon any person,
in connection with the purchase or sale of any security."

[11] Plaintiffs do not specifically discuss this contention in those portions of their memorandum which relate to this part of the motion. Defendants disclaim Section 10(b) liability at pp. 5–8 of their main memorandum; the SEC contends that a Section 10(b) action can be maintained at pp. 7–8 of its brief.

category is composed of those who "aid and abet" or conspire with a party who falls into one of the first three.

In the complaint allegations addressed to the issuance of the allegedly false and misleading annual report, PMM seemingly does not fit into any of the four groupings.[12] The central issue, then, is whether a Section 10(b) action can be maintained against a defendant such as PMM which, so far as appears from the pleadings, did not directly gain from its failure to disclose its discovery of the falsity of the financial statements.

There has been some indication that the factor of gain is an important, if not dispositive, consideration. In Cochran v. Channing Corporation, 211 F.Supp. 239 (S.D.N.Y. 1962), a Section 10(b) civil action was brought against certain directors and a controlling shareholder of a corporation, all of whom were considered "insiders" (211 F.Supp. at 242). One of plaintiff's causes of action was based upon defendants' failure to disclose to the public why the dividends of the corporation had been cut. Judge Dawson ostensibly took the position that nondisclosure alone would not have been sufficient to support the Rule 10b–5 action but had to be accompanied by defendant's use of the information not disclosed. Specifically, it was stated as follows:

> The Securities Exchange Act was enacted in part to afford protection to the ordinary purchaser or seller of securities. Fraud may be accomplished by false statements, a failure to correct a misleading impression left by statements already made or, as in the instant case, by not stating anything at all when there is a duty to come forward and speak. It is the use of the inside information that gives rise to a violation of Rule 10b–5. (211 F.Supp. at 243)

While this statement has been characterized as dictum,[13] it is derived from a statement made by the SEC in Cady, Roberts & Co., 40

---

[12]PMM is alleged to be an aider and abettor for its activity (or inactivity) relating to Yale's issuance of fraudulent interim statements. See discussion infra.

[13]Fleischer, "Federal Corporation Law": An Assessment, 28 Harv.L.Rev. 1146, 1157 n. 51 (1965).

S.E.C. 907 (1961). In that opinion, the Commission found that insiders' obligation to disclose material information rested on two grounds:

> * * * first, the existence of a relationship giving access, directly or indirectly, to information intended to be available only for a corporate purpose and second, the inherent unfairness involved where a party takes advantage of such information knowing that it is unavailable to those with whom he is dealing. (40 S.E.C. at 912)

The rationale of *Cady, Roberts* and Cochran v. Channing Corp. had recently been followed by this court in an important case involving insiders' duty to disclose. Securities and Exchange Comm'n v. Texas Gulf Sulphur Co., 258 F.Supp. 262, 278–281 (S.D.N.Y. Aug. 19, 1966), appeal argued, No. 296, 2d Cir. March 20, 1967.[13a]

All three cases are, of course, distinguishable on their facts from the situation presented by the complaint here. First, none of the three involved nondisclosure in a report required to be filed with the SEC.[14] Second, none dealt with the unique type of nondisclosure alleged on PMM's part. Third, no attempt has been made to characterize PMM as an "insider" and to describe the consequences which might flow therefrom.[15]

Also potentially significant here, because the cases most resembling the facts pleaded by the present plaintiffs have been grounded upon an "aiding and abetting" theory, is the absence of specific assertions that PMM, by its failure to disclose its discovery of the falsity of the financial statements, aided and abetted Yale in defrauding plaintiffs.

In H. L. Green Co. v. Childree, 185 F.Supp. 95 (S.D.N.Y. 1960), defendants were certified public accountants who, according to the complaint, knowingly prepared false financial statements and made other misrepresentations with intent to induce plaintiff to enter into a merger.

[13a]Accord: Kohler v. Kohler Co., 319 F. 2d 634 (7th Cir. 1963).

[14]The possible significance of this is touched upon in Fleischer, supra note 14, at 1156.

[15]See generally Securities & Exchange Comm'n v. Texas Gulf Sulphur, 258 F.Supp. 262, 278–279 (S.D.N.Y. Aug. 19, 1966).

In denying defendants' motion to dismiss the Rule 10b–5 action, the court said, *inter alia:*

> The complaint alleges that these defendants knowingly did acts pursuant to a conspiracy to defraud. Their status as accountants and the fact that their activities were confined to the preparation of false and misleading financial statements and representations does not immunize these defendants from civil suit for their alleged participation. The extent and culpability of that participation must be determined on the trial. (185 F.Supp. at 96)

There is no indication of what approach the court would have taken if the accountants had not been alleged members of a conspiracy to defraud.

In Pettit v. American Stock Exchange, 217 F.Supp. 21 (S.D.N.Y. 1963), plaintiffs pleaded the existence of a conspiracy among all defendants, specifically asserting that the "defendant Exchange and its officers aided, abetted, and assisted the illegal distribution of Swan-Finch stock by failing to take necessary disciplinary action against abusive conduct and practices of which they knew or should have known." 217 F.Supp. at 28. A motion, made by the exchange and other defendants, to dismiss that part of the claim which was based on Section 10(b) was denied on the ground that, "since knowing assistance of or participation in a fraudulent scheme under Section 10(b) gives rise to liability equal to that of the perpetrators themselves, the facts alleged by the trustees, if proven, would permit recovery under Section 10(b)." 217 F.Supp. at 28 (footnote omitted).

As in H. L. Green Co. v. Childree, supra, there was no discussion in *Pettit* of whether a Rule 10b–5 action could have been maintained absent an allegation of conspiracy or aiding and abetting. Such silence, while completely understandable in view of the allegations there set forth, is unfortunate since *Pettit* and the case at bar are analogous in at least two significant respects. First, neither the exchange nor the accounting firm had any economic interest in the transaction involved. Second, both defendants remained inactive in a claimed breach of a duty to disclose at a time when they knew[16] their inaction was having

---

[16]In *Pettit,* it was alleged that the exchange "knew or should have known" of the illegal distribution of the stock in question. 217 F.Supp. at 28.

a detrimental effect on those to whom they owed the duty. It is perhaps arguable that because the defendant exchange in *Pettit* never made any representations upon which an investor could rely, there is theoretically a stronger case against PMM here, even absent allegations of aiding and abetting, in view of the latter's representations in the 1963 annual report.

Another case gives pause for reflection. In Miller v. Bargain City, U.S.A., Inc., 229 F.Supp. 33 (E.D.Pa.1964), defendants were (1) a corporation whose securities plaintiffs had purchased, (2) certain "insiders" of that corporation, (3) an investment house (Bear, Stearns & Co.) and (4) an accounting firm (Laventhol, Krekstein & Co.). Plaintiffs based their claim on alleged violations of Section 10(b) and Rule 10b–5 (Count I) and of the common law (Count II).

The facts alleged were briefly as follows: defendant corporation filed reports and statements with the SEC which were "inaccurate, false, untrue, or misleading." These reports and statements were then reproduced in certain publications of Standard & Poor. Thereafter, relying upon the statements and reports, plaintiff Miller purchased Bargain City stock over-the-counter.

The complaint alleged that all the defendants were liable to the plaintiffs " 'by virtue of a conspiracy with respect to * * * violations' of Section 10(b) of the [Exchange] Act and Rule 10b–5." 229 F.Supp. at 36. A motion to dismiss the Section 10(b) and Rule 10b–5 claim on the grounds that it should have been based exclusively upon Section 18 of the 1934 Act and that there was no "privity" between plaintiffs and defendants was denied.

The court's comments on privity are of some import to our present problem. Since plaintiffs' claim against PMM arose only as a result of the statutory requirement that Yale's annual report be certified by an "independent public accountant," the "semblance of privity" between the parties which was made a requirement to a Section 10(b) action by the court in Joseph v. Farnsworth Radio & Television Corp., 99 F. Supp. 701 (S.D.N.Y.1951), aff'd per curiam, 198 F.2d 883 (2d Cir. 1952) is apparently not present here. In *Bargain City, U.S.A..* there also was no privity or "semblance of privity" since plaintiffs there bought the defendant corporation's stock over the counter, but the court flatly rejected defendant's contention that the action should fail because of lack of privity.

The rationale of the court is persuasive. Judge Lord looked at the statute and at common law principles, neither of which require privity. On the basis of this finding, he concluded:

> In my judgment, it would be an unwarranted constriction of the broad protection contemplated by the federal scheme of securities legislation to engraft upon that scheme a requirement that is neither a part of the statute nor a part of the governing common law tort principles. (229 F.Supp. at 37)

Concluding that this approach is sound, I would refuse to dismiss this Section 10(b) action for lack of privity as that term is usually understood in the law. This is not to say, however, that the specific "connection" or relationship between plaintiffs and PMM is not important here, for this point, as will be seen, is central to this discussion of defendant's liability under Section 10(b) and Rule 10b-5.

The structure of the complaint and the status of the defendants in Miller v. Bargain City, U.S.A., raise several additional considerations which are pertinent. First, can a Section 10(b) action be maintained by a plaintiff against a defendant accountant if there is no allegation of conspiracy? On the basis of the facts described above, this question arises in the same context as that presented in H. L. Green Co. v. Childree, supra. Second, the court in *Bargain City, U.S.A.*, did not refer at all to the fact, if such it was, that any of the defendants benefitted by dint of their alleged malfeasance. Perhaps such a benefit can be assumed to accrue to a corporation when it inflates its financial performance through false or misleading financial statements; perhaps such an allegation of gain is not necessary when the complaint alleges the issuance of false and misleading financial statements; or perhaps there was an allegation of gain but the court did not think any reference to it was necessary to the discussion of the issues of the motion. I hasten to add that I place no weight on the lack of mention of an allegation of gain; rather, I refer to it only because of the interesting questions it raises.

One further facet of *Bargain City, U.S.A.* should be considered. As stated above, plaintiffs there complained of misrepresentations made in reports and statements filed with the SEC by Bargain City and subsequently reproduced in various Standard & Poor publications. Plaintiffs alleged that they purchased Bargain City's securities in reliance upon these reports and statements, which were required by Section 13 of the 1934 Act and by the rules and regulations of the SEC.

In order for an action to be brought under Rule 10b–5, defendant's activities must be "in connection with the purchase or sale of any security." In *Bargain City, U.S.A.,* in spite of an allegation suggesting a clear connection between the alleged misrepresentations and plaintiff's purchase of securities, the court refused to rule on the issue, stating that "it would be premature to attempt here to determine the nature or extent of the connection required by the Act or its sufficiency in this case, for * * * the facts are not crystallized." 229 F.Supp. at 38. While I am not completely convinced that this conservative approach is warranted here, it does suggest that caution should be exercised in deciding the issue, particularly in view of the inadvanced state of discovery in our case.

One other authority should be discussed in relation to the "connection" issue. In Heit v. Weitzen, CCH Fed.Sec.L.Rep. ¶91,701, at 95,577 (S.D.N.Y. June 9, 1966), defendants were the Belock Instrument Corp. and officers and directors thereof. Plaintiff charged that defendants had violated Rule 10b–5(b) by failing to state in Belock's annual report and in various quarterly statements that the corporation's assets were overstated as a result of certain overcharges to the government.

This court found that the alleged fraud was perpetrated against the government and was not "in connection with the purchase or sale of securities," in spite of plaintiffs' allegations that they purchased stock in reliance upon the figures contained in the allegedly false financial statements. Accordingly, a motion to dismiss that part of the complaint based upon Rule 10b–5 was granted.

In the instant case involving a failure to disclose after-acquired information, it is difficult to solve the "connection" issue in terms of

PMM's "purpose." PMM had a very specialized and well-defined task: to audit and to certify Yale's financial statements for the protection of investors. In this sense, all of PMM's energies were directed toward investors. Such was not the case in Heit v. Weitzen where the defrauding of the investors was considered by the court to be secondary to the defrauding of the government.

Neither the conservative approach adopted in Miller v. Bargain City, U.S.A., supra, nor the ruling as to purpose in Heit v. Weitzen are controlling here because of obvious and important factual distinctions. They do, however, point up some of the problems and difficulties inherent in this phase of the motion and are factors which lead me to adopt the approach outlined immediately below.

From the foregoing discussion, it can readily be seen that that branch of PMM's motion to dismiss any claims based on Section 10(b) and Rule 10b–5 raises novel and difficult issues. Because of the importance of the questions involved and the need for further factual and legal development of them by the parties and the SEC, I deem it best to deny this branch of PMM's motion without prejudice to renewal at trial.

II.
Interim Statement Liability

During PMM's conduct of the "special studies" in 1964, Yale utilized its internal accounting procedures to compile figures which could be used to evaluate the company's 1964 performance on a continuing basis. These figures were then inserted in various interim statements and reports issued by Yale, which, Paragraph 22 of the Second Consolidated Amended Complaint alleges, "were widely circulated" and in which there were "gross overstatements" of the company's "earnings and revenues and forecasts thereof."

Plaintiffs claim[17] that PMM is liable for damages suffered as a result of their reliance upon these allegedly false and misleading statements and reports. The argument made by plaintiffs in their memo-

---

[17]The SEC's brief does not discuss PMM's possible liability for its activity, or lack thereof, related to the interim statements.

randum submitted for purposes of this motion can be summarized in the following manner: the dissemination of the interim statements and reports constituted a violation by Yale of Section 10(b) of the 1934 Act in that it was a "manipulative or deceptive device" undertaken "in connection with the purchase or sale" of a security registered on the New York Stock Exchange. PMM knew as a result of its special studies that the figures disseminated were false and misleading but did not disclose its discovery thereof to anyone; moreover, PMM "recommended" to Yale that the false reports be issued. Plaintiffs conclude that, in light of these facts, PMM must be held liable under Section 10(b) for "aiding and abetting" Yale's scheme to defraud its investors. Urging that the complaint fails to succinctly state facts spelling out an actionable conspiracy and contending, that in any event, it owed no duty to the investing public in respect to the special studies, PMM moves to dismiss this claim.[18]

Before undertaking any discussion of the issues raised by these contentions, it should be made clear that I am assuming for the purposes of this motion only that a Section 10(b) cause of action can be maintained against Yale; the merits of such a proposition must await a later determination.[19]

Essentially, plaintiffs claim that PMM aided and abetted Yale in two ways: first, by remaining silent when it was known that the interim reports were false and, second, by recommending or sanctioning the issuance of the reports. There is no allegation that PMM compiled, audited, or certified any of the interim statements, nor is there indication that any of the statements contained material which an investor could justifiably attribute or relate to PMM.

One additional remark should be made by way of introduction to this particular aspect of the defendant's motion to dismiss. There is nothing in the language or legislative history of Section 10(b) of the 1934 Act or in the provisions of Rule 10b–5 which is of significant assistance here. Consequently, I must attempt to reason to a conclusion

---

[18]No express claim of "aiding and abetting" can be found in plaintiffs' complaint. Such a claim is, however, made in plaintiffs' memorandum submitted in opposition to this motion.

[19]For a discussion of the problems raised by this contention, see Fleischer, "Federal Corporation Law": An Assessment, 78 Harv.L.Rev. 1146, 1156–58 (1965).

by application of case law and general principles of tort law. See Brennan v. Midwestern United Life Insurance Co., 259 F.Supp. 673 (N.D.Ind. Sept. 23, 1966).

A. PMM's Silence and Inaction

The issue posed here was stated succinctly by the court in Brennan v. Midwestern United Life Insurance Company, supra:

> Certainly, not everyone who has knowledge of improper activities in the field of securities transactions is required to report such activities. This court does not purport to find such a duty. Yet, duties are often found to arise in the face of special relationships, and there are circumstances under which a person or a corporation may give the requisite assistance or encouragement to a wrongdoer so as to constitute an aiding and abetting by merely failing to take action. * * *
>
> The question raised by the motion at bar is whether the allegations in the complaint will permit evidence which may establish such circumstances in the instant case. (259 F.Supp. at 681–683)

Discussion of two cases in which defendants have been subjected to possible liability as aiders and abettors under Section 10(b) for their silence and inaction is helpful to resolution of this issue.

In Pettit v. American Stock Exchange, 217 F.Supp. 21 (S.D.N.Y. 1963), analyzed heretofore in the discussion relating to PMM's liability attendant to the 1963 annual report, defendant stock exchange and its officers were held accountable for their failure "to take necessary disciplinary action against abusive conduct and practices of which they knew or should have known." 217 F.Supp. at 28.

The case is, however, distinguishable from the one at bar. In Pettit, the exchange was under an independent duty, imposed by Section 6 of the Securities Exchange Act,[20] to adopt and enforce just and equitable principles of trade. Liability was premised, of course, on the breach of that duty.

---

[20]15 U.S.C. § 78f.

No similar independent duty can be found here by application of either statutory or common law principles. Contrary to plaintiffs' suggestion, issuance by Yale of the interim statements created no "special relationship" between the investors and PMM. In respect to the interim statements, PMM was not a statutory "independent public accountant" as it was during the audit and certification of the annual report. PMM made no representations which appeared in the statements, nor did it compile the figures contained therein. In sum, unlike the situation in *Pettit,* there is absolutely no basis in law for imposing upon PMM a duty to disclose its knowledge of the falsity of the interim financial statements.

The discussion of the court in Brennan v. Midwestern United Life Insurance Co., supra, lends support to this conclusion. In that case, defendant was a corporation whose stock was sold by a broker. At the time of suit, the broker was bankrupt. In a class action, plaintiff purchasers of securities alleged that the defendant issuer aided and abetted the broker's violations of Section 10(b) and Rule 10b–5 by failing to disclose to either the SEC or the Indiana Securities Commission that it knew that the broker was making fraudulent representations in the course of the sales and was improperly using the proceeds from the sales.

Defendant moved to dismiss the action on the grounds, *inter alia,* that the complaint failed to state a claim under the "aiding and abetting" theory. The motion was denied. The court reasoned that defendant Midwestern was an "insider" allegedly taking advantage of the broker's activities and, as such, was under a duty to disclose to the investors that the broker was acting improperly. By remaining silent, Judge Eschbach concluded, this duty was breached and the defendant was thereby subject to the "aider and abettor" claim.

As in *Pettit,* defendants' liability was premised upon the rationale that the failure to disclose constituted a breach of duty. But, as indicated, no such duty can be found in the context of those facts pleaded here. Absent such a duty, there is no basis for transforming silence into actionable aiding and abetting.

B. PMM's Acts of Recommending Release of the Statements

Plaintiffs contend that, in addition to failing to disclose that the Yale interim financial statements were false and misleading, PMM actively aided and abetted Yale's alleged violation of Section 10(b) by recommending or sanctioning the release of statements containing figures compiled by Yale's own accountants rather than figures developed by PMM during the course of the special studies. The basis for this claim is said to be found in answers given to plaintiffs' interrogatories (1st Series) by certain individual defendants who are former officers and directors of Yale. Specifically, the following statements are relied upon:

16. Shortly before August 17, 1964, Robert G. Conroy of Peat, Marwick met with defendant Gerald W. Eskow, defendant Fred H. Mackensen and H. Kenneth Sidel at the Bon Vivant restaurant in New York City. At this meeting Mr. Conroy advised Mr. Eskow that the figures shown in the revised Peat, Marwick special study six month report could not be used as the basis of Yale's financial reports for the first half of 1964 and recommended that the corporation release instead the figures prepared by Mr. Mackensen as the head of its internal accounting operation.

17. Mr. Conroy stated that he did not know whether or not Mr. Mackensen's figures were correct and said that the Peat, Marwick special study would not show this even when it was complete. Mr. Conroy also said that basing the six month report upon the Mackensen figures would have the advantage of being consistent with previous reports and that any inaccuracies in these figures would be picked up by Peat, Marwick in the course of its year-end audit at which time any necessary adjustments would be made.

* * * * * *

19. Shortly before November 5, 1964, said Robert G. Conroy [partner of Peat, Marwick] met with defendants Gerald W. Eskow and Fred H. Mackensen and Harold Rosegarten and H. Kenneth Sidel at a luncheon club in the Wall Street area. At this meeting Mr. Conroy told Mr. Eskow that the Peat, Marwick special study report for the first nine months of 1964 could not be used as a basis for Yale's financial reports for this period. Mr. Conroy recommended that these reports be made on the basis of the figures prepared by Mr. Mackensen, once again stating that while he did not know that these figures were accurate he could not say that they were inaccurate either and using them would be inconsistent with earlier reports.

The issue, of course, is whether or not PMM can be termed "aiders and abettors" as a matter of law if the interrogatory answers by certain defendants are established as a matter of fact. Conveniently, the Restatement of Torts provides the following standard by which PMM's putative liability can be measured:

> For harm resulting to a third person from the tortious conduct of another, a person is liable if he
>
> * * * * * *
>
> (b) knows that the other's conduct constitutes a breach of duty and gives substantial assistance or encouragement to the other so to conduct himself. * * * (Restatement, Torts § 876 (1939))

Assuming that PMM knew that Yale was breaching its duty to its investors by issuing false financial statements,[21] the question becomes whether or not PMM gave "substantial assistance or encouragement" to Yale's course of conduct.

From the facts pleaded in the complaint, even when buttressed by the aforementioned answers to interrogatories, it is difficult to characterize PMM's action as "assistance or encouragement" in the sense contemplated by the Restatement. Even if these labels fit the pleaded facts, doubt remains as to whether or not the quantitative term "substantial" could be added to them.

It is, however, inappropriate to make a determination of the "aiding and abetting" issue at this time. Discovery is presently in a relatively inadvanced stage. While plaintiffs can now show only minimal interaction between PMM and Yale in relation to the interim statements, they must be given an opportunity to further explore this facet of the Yale-PMM relationship. "The very fact that this case arises in a newly developing area of law cautions that the court should refrain from

---

[21]Note the Eskows' statement that Mr. Conroy of PMM said that he did not know whether or not the Yale figures were correct. In an affidavit submitted to this court in support of this motion, Mr. Conroy states, *inter alia*.

"Indeed, PMM during 1964 informed Yale's management, from time to time, that the interim figures which Yale's management had released, or was in the process of releasing, were materially different from interim unaudited statements which PMM had compiled from the special studies material. The decision to release the company prepared figures was made solely by management."

abstract and premature legal determinations fashioned in an evidentiary vacuum." Brennan v. Midwestern United Life Ins. Co., 259 F.Supp. at 682.

The cross motion of PMM to dismiss paragraphs 25–25.3 is denied. It is so ordered.

Issues for consideration:

(1) What is the auditor's responsibility when he discovers that financial statements upon which he has previously reported are false and misleading?

(2) What is the significance of the fact that the defendant auditors obtained knowledge of the falsity and inaccuracy of the client's previously issued financial statements while employed to undertake "special studies" for the client's benefit?

(3) What should be the auditor's responsibility for interim unaudited financial statements issued by a client when he has reason to believe they may contain inaccuracies?

(4) Discuss the significance of the following issues in the Yale Express Case:

   a. There was no contractual relationship between the defendant auditors and the plaintiffs.

   b. There was an admitted absence of personal gain on the part of the auditors in their failure to disclose the falsity of the financial statements.

The Continental Vending Machine
Corporation Case

The Continental Vending Machine Corporation Case is an unprecedented case in the area of accountants' legal liability and is certain to have a far reaching impact on the accounting and auditing profession. The United States government indicted several accountants of an internationally known public accounting firm for knowingly drawing up and certifying a false and misleading financial statement. The facts and issues are complex but the more dramatic aspects include convictions for criminal conspiracy and a court judgment on the standards of the profession itself. This case was first tried in the United States District Court for the Southern District of New York and resulted in a hung jury, but upon retrial the defendant auditors were found guilty of criminal conspiracy. The Court of Appeals for the Second Circuit confirmed the lower court and in March 1970 the Supreme Court denied a request for *certiorari*. Included below is the opinion of the Court of Appeals confirming the District Court.

The reader should also review the brief filed by the Institute as *amicus curiae* supporting the petition for a review of the case by the Supreme Court. This brief, published in the May 1970 issue of the *Journal of Accountancy*, contains a lucid delineation of the issues and presents forcefully the profession's position in the case.

United States v. Simon

425 F. 2d 796 (2d Cir. 1969)

Appeal from a judgment of the District Court for the Southern District of New York, Walter R. Mansfield, *Judge*, convicting three defendants, after a verdict, of conspiring to violate 18 U.S.C. §§ 1001 and 1341 and § 32 of the Securities Exchange Act of 1934, 15 U.S.C. § 78 ff., by knowingly drawing up and certifying a false and misleading financial statement of Continental Vending Machine Corporation for the year ending September 30, 1962, and of using the mails to distribute the statement in violation of 18 U.S.C. § 1341. Affirmed.

* * *

FRIENDLY, C. J. . . . Defendant Carl Simon was a senior partner, Robert Kaiser a junior partner, and Melvin Fishman a senior associate in the internationally known accounting firm of Lybrand, Ross Bros. & Montgomery. They stand convicted after trial by Judge Mansfield and a jury in the District Court for the Southern District of New York under three counts of an indictment charging them with drawing up and certifying a false or misleading financial statement of Continental Vending Machine Corporation (hereafter Continental) for the year ending September 30, 1962. After denying motions for acquittal or a new trial, the judge fined Simon $7,000 and Kaiser and Fishman $5,000 each.

Count One of the indictment was for conspiracy to violate 18 U.S.C. §§1001 and 1341 and §32 of the Securities Exchange Act of 1934, 15 U.S.C. §78 ff. Section 1001 provides:

> Whoever, in any matter within the jurisdiction of any department or agency of the United States knowingly and willfully falsifies, conceals or covers up by any trick, scheme, or device a material fact, or makes any false, fictitious or fraudulent statements or representations, or makes or uses any false writing or document knowing the same to contain any false, fictitious or fraudulent statement or entry, shall be fined not more than $10,000 or imprisoned not more than five years or both.

Section 1341 makes criminal the use of the mails in aid of "any scheme or artifice to defraud." Section 32 of the Securities Exchange Act renders criminal the willful and knowing making of a statement in any required report which was false or misleading with respect to any material fact. Counts Three and Six charged two mailings of the statement in violation of 18 U.S.C. §1341. Nothing turns on the different phrasings of the test of criminality in the three statutes. The Government concedes it had the burden of offering proof allowing a reasonable jury to be convinced beyond a reasonable doubt not merely that the financial statement was false or misleading in a material respect but that defendants knew it to be and deliberately sought to mislead.

While every criminal conviction is important to the defendant, there is a special poignancy and a corresponding responsibility on reviewing judges when, as here, the defendants have been men of blameless lives and respected members of a learned profession. See *United States* v. *Kahaner,* 317 F.2d 459, 467 (2 Cir.), *cert. denied,* 375 U.S. 836 (1963). This is no less true because the trial judge, wisely in our view, imposed no prison sentences. On the other hand, as we observed in the *Kahaner* opinion, our office is limited to determining whether the evidence was sufficient for submission to the jury and, if so, whether errors prejudicial to the defendants occurred at the trial.[1]

I.

The trial hinged on transactions between Continental and an affiliate, Valley Commercial Corporation (hereafter "Valley"). The dominant figure in both was Harold Roth, who was president of Continental, supervised the day-to-day operations of Valley, and owned about 25% of the stock of each company.[2]

Valley, which was run by Roth out of a single office on Continental's premises, was engaged in lending money at interest to Continental and others in the vending machine business. Continental would issue negotiable notes to Valley, which would endorse these in blank and use them as collateral for drawing on two lines of credit, of $1 million each, at Franklin National Bank ("Franklin") and Meadowbrook National Bank ("Meadowbrook"), and would then transfer to Continental the discounted amount of the notes. These transactions, beginning as early as 1956, gave rise to what is called "the Valley payable." By the end of fiscal 1962, the amount of this was $1,029,475, of which $543,345 was due within the year.

---

[1] This is an appropriate point for rejecting defendants' argument that it was error to deny their request, opposed by the Government, for a non-jury trial. F.R. Cr. P. 23(a) conditions a non-jury trial on the Government's consent and "does not require that the Government articulate its reasons for demanding a jury trial." *Singer* v. *United States,* 380 U.S. 24, 37 (1965). As we held in *United States* v. *Abrams,* 357 F. 2d 539, 549, *cert. denied,* 384 U.S. 1001 (1966), the complexity of the subject matter of the alleged offense does not alone entitle a defendant to a non-jury trial over the objection of the prosecutor. It is worth noting, although not critical, that the judge doubled the ordinary number of peremptory challenges, and that the jury was highly qualified.

[2] Two other large stockholders of Continental, Forbes and Hirsch, its counsel, Arthur Field, and Roth's father were the remaining principal stockholders of Valley.

In addition to the Valley payable, there was what is known as the "Valley receivable," which resulted from Continental loans to Valley. Most of these stemmed from Roth's custom, dating from mid-1957, of using Continental and Valley as sources of cash to finance his transactions in the stock market.[3] At the end of fiscal 1962, the amount of the Valley receivable was $3.5 million, and by February 15, 1963, the date of certification, it had risen to $3.9 million. The Valley payable could not be offset, or "netted," against the Valley receivable since, as stated, Continental's obligations to Valley were in the form of negotiable notes which Valley had endorsed in blank to the two banks and used as collateral to obtain the cash which it then lent to Continental.

By the certification date, the auditors had learned that Valley was not in a position to repay its debt, and it was accordingly arranged that collateral would be posted. Roth and members of his family transferred their equity in certain securities to Arthur Field, Continental's counsel, as trustee to secure Roth's debt to Valley and Valley's debt to Continental. Some 80% of these securities consisted of Continental stock and convertible debentures.

The 1962 financial statements of Continental, which were dismal by any standard,[4] reported the status of the Valley transactions as follows:

ASSETS

Current Assets:
. . . .
  Accounts and notes receivable:
  . . . .
  Valley Commercial Corp., affiliate (Note 2) $2,143,335
  . . . .
  Noncurrent accounts and notes receivable:
  Valley Commercial Corp., affiliate (Note 2)   1,400,000
  . . . .

---

[3]From mid-1957 until January 1963 Continental thus advanced more than $16 million to Valley and Valley advanced more than $13 million to Roth. Of the latter sum the payment of approximately $6.5 million would have resulted in an overdraft in Valley's account but for the deposit of a Continental check on the same day.

[4]The Company reported an operating loss of $867,000 and write-offs of some $3 million as compared with after-tax profits of $1,249,000 in the preceding year. Even with the inclusion of $2,143,335 of the total Valley receivable of $3,543,335, current assets, $20,102,504, barely exceeded current liabilities, $19,043,262.

LIABILITIES

Current Liabilities:

. . . .

Long-term debt, portion due within one year	$8,203,788
. . . .	
Long-term debt (Note 7)	
. . . .	
Valley Commercial Corp., affiliate (Note 2)	486,130
. . . .	

Notes to Consolidated Financial Statements

2. The amount receivable from Valley Commercial Corp. (an affiliated company of which Mr. Harold Roth is an officer, director
   and stockholder) bears interest at 12% a year. Such amount, less
   the balance of the notes payable to that company, is secured by the
   assignment to the Company of Valley's equity in certain marketable
   securities. As of February 15, 1963, the amount of such equity at
   current market quotations exceeded the net amount receivable.
7. . . . The amounts of long-term debt, including the portion due
   within one year, on which interest is payable currently or has been
   discounted in advance, are as follows:

. . . .

Valley Commercial Corp., affiliate	$1,029,475

The case against the defendants can be best encapsulated by com-
paring what Note 2 stated and what the Government claims it would
have stated if defendants had included what they knew:

2. The amount receivable from Valley Commercial Corp. (an affiliated company of which Mr. Harold Roth is an officer, director
   and stockholder), which bears interest at 12% a year, was uncollectible at September 30, 1962, since Valley had loaned approximately the same amount to Mr. Roth who was unable to pay.
   Since that date Mr. Roth and others have pledged as security for
   the repayment of his obligation to Valley and its obligation to
   Continental (now $3,900,000, against which Continental's liabil-
   ity to Valley cannot be offset) securities which, as of February 15,
   1963, had a market value of $2,978,000. Approximately 80% of
   such securities are stock and convertible debentures of the
   company.

Striking as the difference is, the latter version does not reflect the
Government's further contention that in fact the market value of the

pledged securities on February 15, 1963, was $1,978,000 rather than $2,978,000 due to liens of James Talcott, Inc., and Franklin for indebtedness other than Roth's of which defendants knew or should have known.

II.

Although the facts set forth up to this point were uncontroverted, there were some sharp disagreements concerning just what defendants knew and when they learned it. Issues of credibility, however, were for the jury, and we here set forth what the jury could permissibly have found the further facts to be.

Roth engaged the Lybrand firm as Continental's auditors in 1956. George Shegog was the partner in charge; Simon was "second partner" but had no responsibility save for the review of SEC filings. Upon Shegog's death, early in 1960, Simon became the partner in charge. Kaiser was first assigned to the Continental audit as "audit manager" for the 1961 audit. Fishman had been assigned to the Continental audit in 1957 as a young junior accountant; in 1962 he was promoted to be manager of the Continental audit for that year and Kaiser was retained as "second partner." The day-to-day supervision of the audit was the responsibility of Richard McDevitt. As is usual, the structure was pyramidal in terms of time spent.

The Valley receivable had attracted attention early in Lybrand's engagement. In the late fall of 1958, Yoder, who was then manager of the Continental audit, discussed it with Roth. In a memorandum which was read by Fishman at the time and remained in the Lybrand audit files, Yoder recorded that during fiscal 1958 Continental had made net cash payments to Valley of $1,185,790, which "appeared to be for no other purpose than to provide Valley with cash." He recorded also that since September 30 Continental had made additional payments to Valley of $824,752 which were used "to finance the acquisition of capital stock of U. S. Hoffman Machine Corporation by Mr. Roth, or for loans by Valley to U. S. Hoffman." He also stated that he was informed that the receivable should be applied to notes of Continental and its subsidiaries which represented the Valley payable, and that he had agreed provided that the notes, which Valley had pledged as collateral for its borrowings from Franklin National Bank ("Franklin"), and Meadowbrook National Bank ("Meadowbrook"), were surrendered and made available for Lybrand's inspection. In a memorandum to Simon in November 1960, Yoder again discussed the Valley receivable, noting that the payments were frequent, in round amounts, and unaccompanied by written explanations. He observed that during the 1960 fiscal year the receivable had ranged from $695,000 in October 1959 to $398,000 in September 1960 with a high of $1,583,000 in April 1960.

In 1961 and 1962, the cash payments giving rise to the Valley receivable continued to be frequent, in round amounts, and without written explanation. Moreover, the balance in the Valley receivable account characteristically was parabolic, rising after the end of one fiscal year and falling prior to the end of the next. The payments and repayments and the year-end balances for 1958–1962 are shown by the . . . table [below].

Year	Advances to Valley (E125 329a-376a)	Repayments by Valley (E37 through E49; E127 through E135)	Receivable at Year-End (E1 through E9)
1958	$3,356,239	$2,583,172	$ — 0 —
1959	4,586,000	3,510,451	384,402
1960	2,511,000	2,670,500	397,996
1961	2,390,674	1,520,000	848,006
1962	4,708,000	1,986,500	3,543,335

Although the figure for the end of 1961 was more than double that at the end of the two preceding years, and had increased to about $2 million by December 31, 1961, prior to the certification date, the 1961 financial statement made no comment on the receivable, and none of the defendants asked whether Continental's directors had been informed of the transactions. Simon merely warned Roth that an examination of Valley's books would be required if the receivable at the end of fiscal 1962 was as large as at the end of 1961.

When Fishman visited Continental's office in early September 1962 in preparation for that year's audit, he was told that as of July 31 the Valley receivable had reached $3.6 million. He was told also that Continental was operating a check float in excess of $500,000 daily, that cash was "tighter than ever," and that Continental's Assistant Comptroller had spent most of July and August "juggling cash." Fishman reported this to Simon and Kaiser, noting that "all in all, it promises to be an 'interesting' audit."

The cash audit, conducted in early October 1962, showed how stringent cash had become. The $286,000 in hand on September 30 resulted only from thirty-day-loans of $1.5 million from Franklin and Meadowbrook four days earlier. The Valley receivable was found to be around $3.5 million and Fishman told Roth in late October that this was so large that "there could be a problem with the year-end audit." In answer to a question by Fishman in November why Valley needed so much money, Kalan, Continental's Assistant Comptroller, said that "Roth needed the money to maintain the margin accounts on the U. S. Hoffman stock and bonds and the Continental stock and bonds."

Early in November Fishman met with Kaiser and reviewed the history of the Valley receivable. A memorandum of November 12 from Fishman to Kaiser, with a copy to Simon, "anticipated that September 30, 1962, Continental's balance sheet will show a net receivable from Valley of approximately $1,000,000 representing the excess of cash transfers to Valley over notes issued to Valley" and stated an intention to review the collectibility of the "net receivable" by examining "the latest available financial statements of Valley and other documentation."[5]

In December Fishman phoned Simon that the Valley receivable as of September 30 was about $3.5 million. Simon instructed Fishman to tell Roth that Lybrand would need the financial statements of Valley in order to evaluate the receivable's collectibility. Roth called Simon and said that Valley's audit was not yet finished and that the statements

---

[5]The Government notes that this is the first reference to a netting of the Valley payable against the Valley receivable — something which the defendants concede they knew to be impossible in view of Valley's having pledged Continental's notes as collateral.

would be made available when it was. There were similar conversations during January 1963.

Meanwhile, according to Roth, he had contacted Simon in December and said that although Valley had a net worth of $2 million, it was not in a position to repay its $3.5 million debt to Continental as it had lent him approximately the same amount which he was unable to repay. He suggested that he secure the indebtedness with his equity in stocks, bonds and other securities of Continental and Hoffman International if this would be acceptable. Roth called Simon some ten days later and received the latter's assent. On December 31 Roth placed Arthur Field, counsel for Continental, in charge of preparing the assignments.

Late in January 1963 Fishman visited Roth and showed him a draft of Note 2 substantially identical with the final form; he told Roth that Simon wanted to see him. They met in the Lybrand office on February 6. Defendants concede that at this meeting Roth informed Simon that Valley could not repay Continental and offered to post securities for the Valley receivable, and also to post as collateral a mortgage on his house and furnishings. Simon agreed that if adequate collateral were posted, a satisfactory legal opinion were obtained, and Continental's board approved the transactions, Lybrand could certify Continental's statements without reviewing Valley's, which still were not available. There was also a discussion of verification procedures. Simon determined that Roth, with a Lybrand employee listening on an extension phone, would call the various banks and brokers then holding Roth's securities to confirm the "amount of securities pledged and the amount due to them."

On February 12 Roth told Simon that Field had the collateral ready for verification. Simon instructed Kaiser to go to Field's office. Finding that Field had made the proposed assignments run to Valley, Kaiser called this "ridiculous" and asked, "If the securities or if the cash equity gets back into Valley Commercial Corporation, what is to stop Harold Roth from taking the money out again as he did before?" On Kaiser's direction Field made the assignments run to himself as trustee for Valley and Continental. Field also discussed the available collateral and exhibited to Kaiser some handwritten notes prepared by Field and Miss Gans, secretary to Roth. These showed that the bulk of the collateral would consist of an equity in Continental stock and debentures. Kaiser made a number of calls having reference to this information and prepared notes of them which he later showed Simon; as developed in section V of this opinion, the Government alleges these demonstrated a complete encumbrance of all of Roth's securities held by Franklin, Meadowbrook and James Talcott, Inc. ("Talcott"). At Kaiser's request Field prepared a letter stating that $3.5 million in collateral was being posted and outlining the mechanics of the collateralization. On the following business day Simon called to request that Field amend the letter to include an opinion that the collateral adequately secured the Valley receivable; the amended letter was sent on February 15 or 18. Meanwhile Field had informed Simon and Kaiser on February 13 that Continental's board of directors had disapproved of the loans to Valley.

On Friday, February 15, Kaiser assigned James Harris, a supervisor who had no previous connection with the Continental audit, to confirm the collateral. Kaiser explained the agreed procedure and introduced him to Roth and Miss Gans, but did not warn him of the possibility of encumbrances at Franklin, Meadowbrook and Talcott. The telephone calls began around 10 a.m. and continued until late afternoon when Miss Gans "started having difficulty in reaching some of the people at some of these financial institutions." The calls ended, and Harris totaled the then quoted market price of the confirmed securities, subtracted the indebtedness disclosed over the telephone, and arrived at an equity interest of some $3.1 million, this including an equity of $1.2 million in stock held at Franklin, Meadowbrook and Talcott. He telephoned Kaiser the results. Meanwhile Roth removed some $100,000 in odd securities from an office safe and offered them if Harris didn't have enough. The offer was declined.[6] The schedule was

---

[6]Kaiser subsequently prepared a memorandum of his telephone talk with Harris. This stated that Roth had exhibited a substantial number of loose securities to show that he could bring the collateral up over the promised $3.5 million and that Roth, over the telephone, asked for time to determine which securities would be included in the collateral. The government claimed that this memorandum, which was paginated 79a and 79b as a result of having been inserted between pp. 79 and 80 of the audit files sometime after March 7, 1963, was a fabrication.

then delivered to McDevitt, who applied the closing market quotations of February 15; these reduced the value to $2,978,000.[7]

The three defendants met at Continental's plant on Saturday, February 16, and prepared a printer's draft of the financial statements.[8] Simon telephoned Roth and discussed the proposed statement, including Note 2. In the course of the conversation he requested payment of some $13,000 still owing for the 1961 audit. On Roth's instructions Kalan gave Simon a check, saying "This is going to bounce."

On Monday, February 18, Simon reviewed a printer's proof of the statements. At that time, for reasons which were not developed at trial but are now conceded to be proper, he moved from noncurrent into current assets $1,433,104, representing a receivable from the sale of certain vending routes. At the same time, he dropped from current assets to noncurrent assets some $1,400,000 of the Valley receivable, which Roth caused to be refinanced by Valley's issuance of long-term notes in that amount. Although Simon testified that he made this change solely because of the issuance of the notes, in which he had no part, Roth testified that Simon had earlier told him that some of the $3.5 million Valley receivable would have to go "below the line" — i.e., into noncurrent assets.

---

[7]Defendants claimed that they justifiably relied on Roth's promise that the collateral would include an additional $1,134,960, as follows:

Mortgage on Roth's house and furniture	$ 625,000
Loose stock certificates shown by Roth to Harris	100,000
Equity in U. S. Hoffman Machinery Corp. stock	173,000
Securities listed on schedule shown by Field to Kaiser but not confirmed by Harris	236,960
	$1,134,960

They relied also on Field's opinion letter stating that the receivable was secured by an equity in securities having a value of $3.5 million. However, the first two items were never included in the collateral assigned to Field as trustee. Harris left the U. S. Hoffman Machinery stock out of his list because it had been delisted and had only a nominal quotation of 43¢ per share. Some institutions listed by Field as holding securities were never checked by Harris, but in light of the inaccuracies in Field's list which were revealed by Harris' check, any attempt to evaluate the holdings at these institutions would be highly speculative.

[8]Fishman's handwritten draft of the liability side of the balance sheet showed the current and noncurrent portions of the Valley payable separately from other current and noncurrent liabilities. In revising this draft, Simon included the current portion in a lump sum figure for the total portion of long-term debt payable within a year; however, a reader could determine the current portion by subtracting the long-term debt to Valley from the total shown in Note 7.

The financial statements were mailed as part of Continental's annual report on February 20. By that time the market value of the collateral had declined some $270,000 from its February 15 value. The value of the collateral fell an additional $640,000 on February 21. When the market reopened on February 25 after the long Washington's birthday recess, it fell another $2 million and was worth only $395,000. The same day a Continental check to the Internal Revenue Service bounced. Two days later the Government padlocked the plant and the American Stock Exchange suspended trading in Continental stock. Investigations by the SEC and bankruptcy rapidly ensued.

III.

The defendants called eight expert independent accountants, an impressive array of leaders of the profession. They testified generally that, except for the error with respect to netting, the treatment of the Valley receivable in Note 2 was in no way inconsistent with generally accepted accounting principles or generally accepted auditing standards, since it made all the informative disclosures reasonably necessary for fair presentation of the financial position of Continental as of the close of the 1962 fiscal year. Specifically, they testified that neither generally accepted accounting principles nor generally accepted auditing standards required disclosure of the make-up of the collateral or of the increase of the receivable after the closing date of the balance sheet, although three of the eight stated that in light of hindsight they would have preferred that the make-up of the collateral be disclosed. The witnesses likewise testified that disclosure of the Roth borrowings from Valley was not required, and seven of the eight were of the opinion that such disclosure would be inappropriate. The principal reason given for this last view was that the balance sheet was concerned solely with presenting the financial position of the company under audit; since the Valley receivable was adequately secured in the opinion of the auditors and was broken out and shown separately as a loan to an affiliate with the nature of the affiliation disclosed, this was all that the auditors were required to do. To go further and reveal what Valley had done with the money would be to put into the balance sheet things that did not properly belong there; moreover, it would create a precedent which would imply that it was the duty of an auditor to investigate each loan to an affiliate to determine whether the money had found its way into the pockets of an officer of the company under audit, an investigation that would ordinarily be unduly wasteful of time and money. With due respect to the Government's accounting witnesses, an SEC staff accountant, and, in rebuttal, its chief accountant, who took a contrary view, we are bound to say that they hardly compared with defendants' witnesses in aggregate auditing experience or professional eminence.

Defendants asked for two instructions which, in substance, would have told the jury that a defendant could be found guilty only if, according to generally accepted accounting principles, the financial statements as a whole did not fairly present the financial condition of Continental at September 30, 1962, and then only if his departure from accepted standards was due to willful disregard of those standards with knowledge of the falsity of the statements and an intent to deceive. The judge declined to give these instructions. Dealing with the subject in the course of his charge, he said that the "critical test" was whether the financial statements as a whole "fairly presented the financial position of Continental as of September 30, 1962, and whether it accurately reported the operations for fiscal 1962." If they did not, the basic issue became whether defendants acted in good faith. Proof of compliance with generally accepted standards was "evidence which may be very persuasive but not necessarily conclusive that he acted in good faith, and that the facts as certified were not materially false or misleading. . . . The weight and credibility to be extended by you to such proof, and its persuasiveness, must depend, among other things, on how authoritative you find the precedents and the teachings relied upon by the parties to be, the extent to which they contemplate, deal with, and apply to the type of circumstances found by you to have existed here, and the weight you give to expert opinion evidence offered by the parties. Those may depend on the credibility extended by you to expert witnesses, the definiteness with which they testified, the reasons given for their opinions, and all the other facts affecting credibility . . ."

Defendants contend that the charge and refusal to charge constituted error. We think the judge was right in refusing to make the accountants' testimony so nearly a complete defense. The critical test according to the charge was the same as that which the accountants testified was critical. We do not think the jury was also required to accept the accountants' evaluation whether a given fact was material to overall fair presentation, at least not when the accountants' testimony was not based on specific rules or prohibitions to which they could point, but only on the need for the auditor to make an honest judgment and their conclusion that nothing in the financial statements themselves negated the conclusion that an honest judgment had been made. Such evidence may be highly persuasive, but it is not conclusive, and so the trial judge correctly charged.

Defendants next contend that, particularly in light of the expert testimony, the evidence was insufficient to allow the jury to consider the failure to disclose Roth's borrowings from Valley, the make-up of the collateral, or the post balance sheet increase in the Valley receivable. They concentrate their fire on what they characterize as the "primary, predominant and pervasive" issue, namely the failure to disclose that Continental's loans to Valley were not for a proper business purpose but to assist Roth in his personal financial problems. It was "primary, predominant and pervasive" not only because it was most featured by the prosecution but because defendants' knowledge of Roth's diversion of corporate funds colored everything else. We join defendants' counsel in assuming that the mere fact that a company has made advances to an affiliate does not ordinarily impose a duty on an accountant to investigate what the affiliate has done with them or even to disclose that the affiliate has made a loan to a common officer if this has come to his attention. But it simply cannot be true that an accountant is under no duty to disclose what he knows when he has reason to believe that, to a material extent, a corporation is being operated not to carry out its business in the interest of all the stockholders but for the private benefit of its president. For a court to say that all this is immaterial as a matter of law if only such loans are thought to be collectible would be to say that independent accountants have no responsibility to reveal known dishonesty by a high corporate officer. If certification does not at least imply that the corporation has not been looted by insiders so far as the accountants know, or, if it has been, that the diversion has been made good beyond peradventure (or adequately reserved against) and effective steps taken to prevent a recurrence, it would mean nothing, and the reliance placed on it by the public would be a snare and a delusion. Generally accepted accounting principles instruct an accountant what to do in the usual case where he has no reason to doubt that the affairs of the corporation are being honestly conducted. Once he has reason to believe that this basic assumption is false, an entirely different situation confronts him. Then, as the Lybrand firm stated in its letter accepting the Continental engagement, he must "extend his procedures to determine whether or not such suspicions are justified." If as a result of such an extension or, as here, without it, he finds his suspicions to be confirmed, full disclosure must be the rule, unless he has made sure the wrong has been righted and procedures to avoid a repetition have been established. At least this must be true when the dishonesty he has discovered is not some minor peccadillo but a diversion so large as to imperil if not destroy the very solvency of the enterprise.

On this dominating issue of Roth's diverting corporate funds we do not have a case where the question is whether accountants may be subjected to criminal sanction for closing their eyes to what was plainly to be seen. Fishman was proved to have known what was going on since 1958, Simon must have had a good idea about it from the spring of 1960 when Roth informed him that he had borrowed $1,000,000 from investment bankers to make a repayment to Valley, and the jury could infer that Kaiser also was not unaware. If Roth's testimony was believed, the defendants knew almost all the facts from December 1962. In any event they concede knowledge prior to the certification. Beyond what we have said, Field testified that at a meeting in February 1963 before the statements were certified, he, Simon and Kaiser discussed "how was it possible for a man like Harold Roth . . . for a man like that to go wrong and to take out this money through the circuitous method of having it first go into Valley and then to withdraw it immediately by himself . . ." The jury could reasonably have wondered how accountants who were really seeking to tell the truth could have constructed a footnote so well designed to conceal the shocking facts. This was not simply by the lack of affirmative disclosure but by the failure to describe the securities under circumstances crying for a disclosure and the failure to press Roth for a mortgage on his house and furnishings, description of which in the footnote would necessarily have indicated the source of the collateral and thus evoked inquiry where the money advanced to Valley had gone.

Turning to the failure to describe the collateral, defendants concede that they could not properly have certified statements showing the Valley receivable as an asset when they knew it was uncollectible. That was why Roth proposed collateralization and they accepted it. As men experienced in financial matters, they must have known that the one kind of property ideally unsuitable to collateralize a receivable whose collectibility was essential to avoiding an excess of current liabilities over current assets and a two-thirds reduction in capital already reduced would be securities of the very corporation whose solvency was at issue — particularly when the 1962 report revealed a serious operating loss. Failure to disclose that 80% of the "marketable securities" by which the Valley receivable was said to be "secured"[9] were securities of Continental was thus altogether unlike a failure to state how much collateral were bonds or stocks of General Motors and how much of U. S. Steel. Indeed one of the defense experts testified that disclosure would be essential if Continental stock constituted more than 50% of the collateral. Beyond this, we are not here required to determine whether failure to reveal the nature of the collateral would have been a submittable issue if the Valley receivable had constituted an advance made for a legitimate business purpose. Defendants' conduct had to be judged in light of their failure to reveal the looting by Roth. Since disclosure that 80% of the securities were Continental stock or debentures would have led to inquiry who could furnish so much, the jury could properly draw the inference that the

---

[9]A Lybrand practice bulletin warned against use of the word "secured" since the ordinary reader would regard this as meaning "fully secured."

failure to reveal that the bulk of the pledged securities was of the one sort most inappropriate to "secure" the Valley receivable, rather than being a following of accepted accounting principles, was part of a deliberate effort to conceal what defendants knew of the diversion of corporate funds that Roth had perpetrated.

We are likewise unimpressed with the argument that defendants cannot be charged with criminality for failure to disclose the known increase in the Valley receivable from $3.4 to $3.9 million. Here again the claim that generally accepted accounting practices do not require accountants to investigate and report on developments since the date of the statements being certified has little relevance. Note 2 stated "As of February 15, 1963, the amount of such equity at current market quotations exceeded the net amount receivable." This means the net amount receivable as of February 15. If the receivable remained at the $3.9 million level it had attained at December 31, 1962, and there is nothing to indicate its reduction, the collateral of $2.9 million verified by Harris barely equalled even the "net" receivable, since the collateral, supplied long after September 30, 1962, although this also was not disclosed, concededly was security for advances after September 30 as well as before. The jury was thus entitled to infer that the failure to reveal the increase in the Valley receivable was part of an effort to create an appearance of collectibility which defendants knew to be false. Indeed one of the defense experts agreed that the increase in the receivable was a material event that required disclosure in the absence of sufficient collateral. Moreover, this issue, like the others, must be considered in context. The jury could find that failure to reveal the known increase in the Valley receivable, rather than being motivated by adherence to accepted accounting principles, was due to fear that revelation of the increase would arouse inquiry why a company in the desperate condition of Continental would go on advancing money to an affiliate and thus lead to discovery of Roth's looting.

IV.

Defendants properly make much of the alleged absence of proof of motivation. They say that even if the Government is not bound to show evil motive, and we think it is not, see *Pointer* v. *United States*, 151 U.S. 396 (1894), lack of evidence of motive makes the burden of proving criminal intent peculiarly heavy and the Government did not discharge this.

It is quite true that there was no proof of motive in the form usual in fraud cases. None of the defendants made or could make a penny from Continental's putting out false financial statements. Neither was there evidence of motive in the sense of fear that telling the truth would lose a valuable account. Continental was not the kind of client whose size would give it leverage to bully a great accounting firm, nor was it important to the defendants personally in the sense of their having brought in the business. One would suppose rather that the Continental account had become a considerable headache to the Lybrand firm generally and to the defendants in particular; they could hardly have been unaware of the likelihood that the many hours the firm had devoted to the 1962 audit would not be compensated and that another might never occur. Ordinary commercial motivation is thus wholly absent.

The Government finds motive in defendants' desire to preserve Lybrand's reputation and conceal the alleged dereliction of their predecessors and themselves in former years — the failure to advise Continental's board of directors of Roth's role in creating the Valley receivable, see N.Y. Stock Corporation Law § 59; the failure to expand the scope of the audit for those years to determine the nature and collectibility of the Valley receivable, despite the injunction in a well-known text originally authored by one of the founders of the Lybrand firm, that receivables from affiliates must be scrutinized carefully to determine they "are what they purport to be;"[10] and the certification of the 1961 statements despite Simon's warning to Roth that a further increase in the receivable would necessitate an examination of Valley's books. The apparent failure of the defendants to consult with the Lybrand executive committee, or with the partner in the firm to whom "problems" in audits were supposed to be referred, on what would

---

[10]Montgomery, *Auditing,* 180. Simon had contributed to a revision of this standard work.

seem highly important policy questions concerning the 1962 audit adds force to these arguments.

The main response is that if the defendants had wanted to cover up any past delinquencies they would not have insisted on financial statements so dismal in other respects. It is alleged that defendants demanded certain adjustments which good accounting practice permitted but did not require. It is said also that defendants must have known the statements were so unfavorable, even with the limited disclosure in Note 2, that Continental was bound to fold and a full investigation would follow. The argument is impressive but not dispositive. Defendants may have harbored the illusion that the dexterity of Continental's treasurer in "juggling cash" would enable it to survive. Moreover, men who find themselves in a bad situation of their own making do not always act with full rationality.

Even if there were no satisfactory showing of motive, we think the Government produced sufficient evidence of criminal intent. Its burden was not to show that defendants were wicked men with designs on anyone's purse, which they obviously were not, but rather that they had certified a statement knowing it to be false. As Judge Hough said for us long ago, "while there is no allowable inference of knowledge from the mere fact of falsity, there are many cases where from the actor's special situation and continuity of conduct an inference that he did know the untruth of what he said or wrote may legitimately be drawn." *Bentel* v. *United States,* 13 F.2d 327, 329, *cert. denied,* 273 U.S. 713 (1926). See also *Aiken* v. *United States,* 108 F.2d 182, 183 (4 Cir. 1939). Moreover, so far as criminal intent is concerned, the various deficiencies in the footnote should not be considered in isolation. Evidence that defendants knowingly suppressed one fact permitted, although it surely did not compel, an inference that their suppression of another was likewise knowing and willful.

In addition to all that has been said on this score in the previous section of this opinion, a strong indication of knowing suppression lay in the evidence concerning the erroneous reduction of the Valley receivable by the $1 million of notes payable. Defendants say that this was mere negligence; that, beginning with Fishman's memorandum of November 12, 1962, they were "thinking net." But the jury was not bound to accept this. Even if the jury believed that Fishman had negligently slipped into error in November 1962,[11] despite his peculiar awareness of the impossibility of netting, which it was not required to do, it truly taxed credulity to suppose that, with all the attention that was given to the Valley receivable over the next three months, none of these defendants, experienced in the business of Continental, ever mentioned to the others that the critical figure was not the net receivable but the gross, as indeed the body of the financial statements showed, so that $3 million of collateral would not secure the receivable. Indeed Simon and Kaiser swore in depositions taken in a civil suit brought by Continental's bankruptcy Trustee and before the grand jury that they had known in February 1963 that the Continental notes were pledged so that netting was impossible, and made the implausible contention, as did Fishman in his grand jury testimony, that Note 2 had not netted. Defendants' attempt to escape from all this by alleging that they learned of the pledges of the Continental notes only in discussions with a Valley employee in May 1963, may have made matters worse for them with the jury rather than better. For the employee denied the conversation and the story was inconsistent with the failure to net in the financial statements themselves and with other evidence.

The Government furnished added evidence of criminal intent in the shape of conflicting statements by the defendants and contradictions by other witnesses. Simon and Fishman had testified before the Referee in Continental's bankruptcy proceedings that they had discussed, together with Kaiser, whether disclosure need be made of the nature of the collateral, and had rejected this as unnecessary. Yet Simon testified at trial that no consideration had been given to this and Fishman could not recall any discussion. Simon and Fishman swore to the Referee that they had not known of Roth's borrowings from Valley until March 1963. On the other hand, Fishman admitted before the grand jury that he had known of them as early as 1958; Roth testified to telling Simon about them in December 1962; all the defendants now admit they were fully informed before the certification in February

---

[11]The memorandum of November 12 is peculiar in that it refers to the anticipated net figure as approximately $1 million although the gross receivable at July 30, 1962, was known to be $3.6 million and the payable to run to some $1 million yearly. Fishman hadn't "the slightest idea" where the $1 million net figure came from.

1963; and counsel for Continental's trustee testified that Simon had admitted knowing the facts "a long time" before that. When we add the delay in getting at the critical matter of the Valley receivable, the failure to follow up Roth's offer of a mortgage on his house and furniture, and the last minute changes in the balance sheet, we find it impossible to say that a reasonable jury could not be convinced beyond a reasonable doubt that the striking difference between what Note 2 said and what it needed to say in order to reveal the truth resulted not from mere carelessness but from design. That some other jury might have taken a more lenient view, as the trial judge said he would have done, is a misfortune for the defendants but not one within our power to remedy.

V.

In this last section of the opinion we will treat defendants' arguments concerning securities of Roth held by Franklin and Talcott, and the judge's handling of questions by the jury on this and another matter.

Kaiser's notes of his interview of February 12, 1963, with Field, which he showed to Simon on the next day, contained [a list of these securities is shown below].

[Subtotal] $1,293

"Harold Roth"	645,000 shs. Cont. Vend. common Market 2-11-63 — 4⅛	$2,660M
	24,000 shs. Hoffman Int'l common Market 2-11-63 — 3⅝	87
		$2,747M

"Above is pledged as follows:

"Talcott & banks primary security is third party paper"	James Talcott — 200,000 shs. Cont. Vend. com. securing Cont. Vend. & U. S. Hoffman borrowing
	Franklin Natl. & Meadowbrook Banks 445,000 shs. Cont. Vend. common 24,000 shs. Hoffman Int. com. } securing Valley borrowing (1MM from each bank)

Valley will give Cont. Vend. a letter stating that upon payment of Talcott & Bank borrowing, above stock will not be disposed of except to repay Valley's note to Cont. Vend. 2.747

$4,040"

Neither Kaiser nor Field communicated to Harris this indication that the securities held by Franklin, Meadowbrook and Talcott were subject to liens arising from borrowings other than Roth's. When Roth called Meadowbrook, with Harris listening on an extension phone, the bank stated that it held 23,600 shares of Hoffman International stock worth $80,000 which was "Security on Valley obligation," as it later confirmed in writing. Although Harris recorded this on his worksheet, he nevertheless included the $80,000 in the collateral, which defendants admit to have been an error although assertedly an inconsequential one. Franklin said it held 144,484 shares of U. S. Hoffman, 24,411 of Hoffman International and 585,600 of Continental against a loan of $1,525,000 to Roth, as it subsequently confirmed in writing. Harris' computation, as later revised by McDevitt, included an equity of $900,000 in these securities. There was an erasure, innocent on defendants' view, in the "Comments" column of Harris' worksheets in regard to Franklin. The worksheets with respect to Talcott showed a holding of 67,000 Continental shares as "Collateral on indebtedness of Con. Vend. Mach. to Hoffman Mach." Harris included these shares at $270,000, their full market value. Harris' report did not show to whom he had talked at Talcott, and no written confirmation was received.[12]

The Government was allowed to prove by internal records of Franklin that the securities there constituted collateral for Valley's debt of $944,269 in addition to Roth's personal debt. It was also allowed to prove by internal records of Talcott that Roth had pledged 25,000 Continental shares to secure the payment of Hoffman International notes discounted by U. S. Hoffman and 40,000 shares to guarantee loans by Talcott to Crescent Vending, a total liability exceeding $1 million. The court made clear to the jury that the contention was not that defendants had seen the Franklin or Talcott records but rather that "they should have known, and shut their eyes to the inquiry." Defendants contend that even this limited use of the records was improper.

---

[12]In his deposition in the trustee's suit Harris had testified to a vague recollection that he had included these securities because Roth had wanted them included and had indicated an intention to replace them at Talcott with other collateral, to wit, his home.

We have little difficulty in sustaining the court's ruling with respect to Kaiser and Simon. Kaiser's interview with Field, the notes of which were shown to Simon, indicated the unavailability of the securities held at the two banks and Talcott. The jury could take the failure to pass this information on to Harris and the acceptance of his schedules without further inquiry despite their confirmation of the unavailability of the stock at Meadowbrook and Talcott to be evidence of willingness to be satisfied with anything that would create the appearance of adequate security. Although defendants contend that the force of Kaiser's notes of February 12 was dissipated by another schedule given by Field allegedly on February 14 (which the Government disputes), making no reference to liens arising from indebtedness other than Roth's, this was a matter for the jury. The effect of Franklin's confirmation is dissolved if the only question propounded to it was the amount of Roth's indebtedness; furthermore the jury was not required to accept the innocent explanation of the erasure. As to Kaiser and Simon the Government was thus entitled to show, under proper instructions, what proper inquiry would have revealed. On the other hand the evidence would have been admissible against Fishman only on the basis that, his membership in a conspiracy having been sufficiently shown, further evidence of the derelictions of the other conspirators was also admissible against him. While he would have been entitled to an instruction making that clear, none was sought.

During the evening after the case was submitted, the jury, which had been conferring for several hours, reported it was deadlocked, but the judge instructed it to deliberate further. Before leaving the courtroom it then asked three questions:

" 'Is there evidence, undisputed or otherwise that the $2.9 million collateral had prior liens?'

"That is question No. 1.

"Question No. 2:

" 'Where did the proceeds of the home and furnishings mortgage go?'

"Now 3:

" 'Was there testimony to the effect that the $2,900,000 was reduced to $1,700,000?' "

After an endeavor to answer these had led to extended colloquy, the judge dismissed the jury for the night, heard counsel again the next morning, and then addressed the jury.

Instead of answering the first question categorically, the judge made a painstaking summary of all the evidence in which he developed the conflicting contentions and the inferences the jury could draw or not as it saw fit. With a single exception discussed in the margin,[13] defendants make no criticism of the summary, and we can find no basis for any. The judge then said he would defer answering the third question because he did not understand the meaning of the words "reduced to." While it might have been better if the judge had simply referred back to what he had already said, we see no error of which the defendants can complain. The judge's detailed answer to the first question provided the best possible assistance with respect to the third, and he could not properly have given the categorical negative answer the defendants desired.[14]

We likewise see no basis for criticizing the judge's answering of the second question by reading to the jury the relevant testimony of Simon and Field. This made clear that, although Roth had assigned the mortgages to Valley and Continental ultimately received them, they were not included in the collateral for the payment of the Valley receivable which constituted the basis for defendants' assertion of adequate collateralization.

---

[13]Defendants contend the judge should have instructed that the Continental shares pledged with Talcott were good collateral as a matter of law despite Talcott's lien on them to secure what Kaiser's schedule reflected as a Continental note to U. S. Hoffman. The argument, which the judge fairly presented to the jury, is that if Continental paid the note, it would receive the collateral, whereas if it did not pay, it would get the advantage of application of the collateral in reduction of the note without Roth's being subrogated to Talcott's claim for that amount. However, the jury could find that the prospect of Continental's paying the note was remote and that the availability of collateral to reduce a liability of Continental did not make it proper security for the collectibility of the Valley receivable. Furthermore, the true facts, revealed in Harris' worksheets, were that the stock was security for a liability not of Continental but of two other companies.

[14]Defendants likewise complain that the judge did not develop that there may have been collateral in addition to the $2.9 million reflected in Harris' worksheets and McDevitt's revision, see fn. 7. But the questions were framed by the jury and defendants made no request for the judge to deal with this point.

We have carefully reviewed the few other arguments made by the defendants but do not consider them of sufficient importance to justify prolonging this already long opinion. This was a trial bitterly but honorably fought, by exceedingly capable and well-prepared counsel, before an able judge experienced in complicated litigation and a highly intelligent jury. Finding that the evidence was sufficient for submission to the jury and that no legal errors were committed, we must let the verdict stand.

Affirmed.

Issues for consideration:

(1) Discuss the issue of the criminal conviction of the defendants in the case. What are the implications for auditors generally?

(2) What is the significance of the court's refusal to instruct the jury to find the auditors guilty only if the financial statements did not present fairly financial conditions according to *generally accepted accounting principles?*

(3) What were the deficiencies in audit procedures brought out in this case? Should the accounting profession develop more explicit audit procedures to guide the auditor?

The BarChris Construction Corporation Case

The BarChris Case, which the *Journal of Accountancy* (June, 1968) calls a landmark decision on liability, is a class action under the Securities Act of 1933 brought by sixty-five purchasers of BarChris' debentures against accountants and others, including underwriters, legal counsel, officers and directors. All defendants, including the auditors, were found to have not established an adequate defense. In this case the court made a searching inquiry leading to definite conclusions as to the adequacy of specific auditing procedures, accounting principles and reporting problems. Further, the court ruled on "materiality," and placed great stress upon the importance of the review of events subsequent to the date of the audited balance sheet.

Reproduced below are excerpts from the court's opinion which provide some background as to the facts in the case and which relate to the defendant auditors. The case was subsequently settled through agreement by the defendants to pay certain sums to the plaintiffs.

Escott v. BarChris Construction Corporation

283 F. Supp. 643 (S.D.N.Y. 1968)

MCLEAN, D. J. . . . This is an action by purchasers of 5½ percent convertible subordinated fifteen year debentures of BarChris Construction Corporation (BarChris). Plaintiffs purport to sue on their own behalf and "on behalf of all other and present and former holders" of the debentures. When the action was begun on October 25, 1962, there were nine plaintiffs. Others were subsequently permitted to intervene. At the time of the trial, there were over sixty.

The action is brought under Section 11 of the Securities Act of 1933 (15 U.S.C. § 77k). Plaintiffs allege that the registration statement with respect to these debentures filed with the Securities and Exchange Commission, which became effective on May 16, 1961, contained material false statements and material omissions.

Defendants fall into three categories: (1) the persons who signed the registration statement; (2) the underwriters, consisting of eight investment banking firms, led by Drexel & Co. (Drexel);[1] and (3) BarChris' auditors, Peat, Marwick, Mitchell & Co. (Peat, Marwick).

* * *

Defendants, in addition to denying that the registration statement was false, have pleaded the defenses open to them under Section 11 of the Act, plus certain additional defenses, including the statute of limitations. Defendants have also asserted cross-claims against each other, seeking to hold one another liable for any sums for which the respective defendants may be held liable to plaintiffs.

This opinion will not concern itself with the cross-claims or with issues peculiar to any particular plaintiff. These matters are reserved for later decision. On the main issue of liability, the questions to be decided are (1) did the registration statement contain false statements of fact, or did it omit to state facts which should have been stated in order to prevent it from being misleading; (2) if so, were the facts which were falsely stated or omitted "material" within the meaning of the Act; (3) if so, have defendants established their affirmative defenses?

* * *

Peat, Marwick, BarChris' auditors, who had previously audited BarChris' annual balance sheet and earnings figures for 1958 and 1959, did the same for 1960. These figures were set forth in the registration statement. In addition, Peat, Marwick undertook a so-called "S-1 review," the proper scope of which is one of the matters debated here.

The registration statement in its final form contained a prospectus as well as other information. Plaintiffs' claims of falsities and omissions pertain solely to the prospectus, not to the additional data.

The prospectus contained, among other things, a description of BarChris' business, a description of its real property, some material

---

[1]The action has been severed as against one underwriter, Ira Haupt & Co., which is in bankruptcy.

pertaining to certain of its subsidiaries, and remarks about various other aspects of its affairs. It also contained financial information. It included a consolidated balance sheet as of December 31, 1960, with elaborate explanatory notes. These figures had been audited by Peat, Marwick. It also contained unaudited figures as to net sales, gross profit and net earnings for the first quarter ended March 31, 1961, as compared with the similar quarter for 1960. In addition, it set forth figures as to the company's backlog of unfilled orders as of March 31, 1961, as compared with March 31, 1960, and figures as to BarChris' contingent liability, as of April 30, 1961, on customers' notes discounted and its contingent liability under the so-called alternative method of financing.

Plaintiffs challenge the accuracy of a number of these figures. They also charge that the text of the prospectus, apart from the figures, was false in a number of respects, and that material information was omitted. Each of these contentions, after eliminating duplications, will be separately considered.[2]

* * *

Summary

For convenience, the various falsities and omissions which I have discussed in the preceding pages are recapitulated here. They were as follows:

1. *1960 Earnings*

    (a) *Sales*

As per prospectus	$9,165,320
Correct figure	8,511,420
Overstatement	$ 653,900

---

[2]The testimony on many subjects in this case is confused. It is scattered over some 6,500 pages of stenographic minutes without any coherent explanation all in one place. To some extent this was inevitable, in view of the number of defendants, each of whom cross-examined the witnesses, plus the fact that plaintiffs, for the most part, were compelled to prove their case out of the mouths of hostile witnesses. I have examined this material, but there is no need to recount it in great detail in this opinion. On each issue I shall state plaintiffs' contention and my findings of fact with respect to it, which are based upon all the evidence related to that issue.

(b) *Net Operating Income*

As per prospectus $1,742,801
Correct figure 1,496,196
Overstatement .... $ 246,605

(c) *Earnings per Share*

As per prospectus .... $.75
Correct figure .... .65
Overstatement .... $.10

2. *1960 Balance Sheet*

Current Assets

As per prospectus $4,524,021
Correct figure 3,914,332
Overstatement .... $ 609,689

3. *Contingent Liabilities as of December 31, 1960 on Alternative Method of Financing*

As per prospectus .... $ 750,000
Correct figure 1,125,795
Understatement .... $ 375,795
Capitol Lanes should have been shown as a direct liability .... $ 325,000

4. *Contingent Liabilities as of April 30, 1961*

As per prospectus .... $ 825,000
Correct figure 1,443,853
Understatement .... $ 618,853
Capitol Lanes should have been shown as a direct liability .... $ 314,166

5. *Earnings Figures for Quarter Ending March 31, 1961*

(a) *Sales*

As per prospectus $2,138,455
Correct figure 1,618,645
Overstatement .... $ 519,810

CASE NO. 41

(b) *Gross Profit*

As per prospectus .... $ 483,121
Correct figure 252,366
Overstatement .... $ 230,755

6. *Backlog as of March 31, 1961*

As per prospectus $6,905,000
Correct figure 2,415,000
Overstatement $4,490,000

7. *Failure to Disclose Officers' Loans Outstanding and Unpaid on May 16, 1961* .... $ 386,615

8. *Failure to Disclose Use of Proceeds in Manner not Revealed in Prospectus*
Approximately $1,160,000

9. *Failure to Disclose Customers' Delinquencies in May 1961 and BarChris' Potential Liability with Respect Thereto* .... Over $1,350,000

10. *Failure to Disclose the Fact that BarChris Was Already Engaged, and Was About to Be More Heavily Engaged, in the Operation of Bowling Alleys*

Materiality

It is a prerequisite to liability under Section 11 of the Act that the fact which is falsely stated in a registration statement, or the fact that is omitted when it should have been stated to avoid misleading, be "material." The regulations of the Securities and Exchange Commission pertaining to the registration of securities define the word as follows (17 C.F.R. § 230.405(1)):

"The term 'material,' when used to qualify a requirement for the furnishing of information as to any subject, limits the information required to those matters as to which an average prudent investor ought reasonably to be informed before purchasing the security registered."

What are "matters as to which an average prudent investor ought reasonably to be informed"? It seems obvious that they are matters which such an investor needs to know before he can make an intelligent, informed decision whether or not to buy the security.

Early in the history of the Act, a definition of materiality was given in *Matter of Charles A. Howard,* 1 S. E. C. 6, 8 (1934), which is still valid today. A material fact was there defined as:

". . . a fact which if it had been correctly stated or disclosed would have deterred or tended to deter the average prudent investor from purchasing the securities in question."

Cf. List v. *Fashion Park, Inc.,* 340 F. 2d 457, 462 (2d Cir. 1965), cert. denied, 382 U.S. 811 (1965) (Securities Exchange Act of 1934 § 10(b))

Restatement of Torts § 538(2)(a)(1938)

Restatement (Second) of Torts § 402B comment g (1965)

The average prudent investor is not concerned with minor inaccuracies or with errors as to matters which are of no interest to him. The facts which tend to deter him from purchasing a security are facts which have an important bearing upon the nature or condition of the issuing corporation or its business.

Judged by this test, there is no doubt that many of the misstatements and omissions in this prospectus were material. This is true of all of them which relate to the state of affairs in 1961, *i.e.,* the overstatement of sales and gross profit for the first quarter, the understatement of contingent liabilities as of April 30, the overstatement of orders on hand and the failure to disclose the true facts with respect to officers' loans, customers' delinquencies, application of proceeds and the prospective operation of several alleys.

The misstatements and omissions pertaining to BarChris' status as of December 31, 1960, however, present a much closer question. The 1960 earnings figures, the 1960 balance sheet and the contingent liabilities as of December 31, 1960 were not nearly as erroneous as plaintiffs have claimed. But they were wrong to some extent, as we have seen. Would it have deterred the average prudent investor from purchasing these debentures if he had been informed that the 1960 sales were $8,511,420 rather than $9,165,320, that the net operating income was $1,496,196 rather than $1,742,801 and that the earnings per share in 1960 were approximately 65¢ rather than 75¢? According to the unchallenged figures, sales in 1959 were $3,320,121 net operating income was $441,103, and earnings per share were 33¢. Would it have made a difference to an average prudent investor if he had known that in 1960 sales were only 256 percent of 1959 sales, not 276 percent; that net operating income was up by only 1,055,093, not by $1,301,698, and that earnings per share, while still approximately twice those of 1959, were not something more than twice?

These debentures were rated "B" by the investment rating services. They were thus characterized as speculative, as any prudent investor must have realized. It would seem that anyone interested in buying these convertible debentures would have been attracted primarily by the conversion feature, by the growth potential of the stock. The growth which the company enjoyed in 1960 over prior years was striking, even on the correct figures. It is hard to see how a prospective purchaser of this type of investment would have been deterred from buying if he had been advised of these comparatively minor errors in reporting 1960 sales and earnings.

Since no one knows what moves or does not move the mythical "average prudent investor," it comes down to a question of judgment, to be exercised by the trier of the fact as best he can in the light of all the circumstances. It is my best judgment that the average prudent investor would not have cared about these errors in the 1960 sales and earnings figures, regrettable though they may be. I therefore find that they were not material within the meaning of Section 11.

The same is true of the understatement of contingent liabilities in footnote 9 by approximately $375,000. As disclosed in that footnote, BarChris's contingent liability as of December 31, 1960 on notes discounted was $3,969,835 and, according to the footnote, on the alternative method of financing was $750,000, a total of $4,719,835. This was a huge amount for a company with total assets, as per balance sheet, of $6,101,085. Purchasers were necessarily made aware of this by the figures actually disclosed. If they were willing to buy the debentures in the face of this information, as they obviously were, I doubt that they would have been deterred if they had been told that the contingent liabilities were actually $375,000 higher.

This leaves for consideration the errors in the 1960 balance sheet figures which have previously been discussed in detail. Current assets were overstated by approximately $600,000.[3] Liabilities were understated by approximately $325,000 by the failure to treat the liability on Capitol Lanes as a direct liability of BarChris on a consolidated basis. Of this $325,000 approximately $65,000, the amount payable on Capitol within one year, should have been treated as a current liability.

As per balance sheet, cash was $285,482. In fact, $145,000 of this had been borrowed temporarily from Talcott and was to be returned by January 16, 1961 so that realistically, cash was only $140,482. Trade accounts receivable were overstated by $150,000 by including Howard Lanes Annex, an alley which was not sold to an outside buyer.

As per balance sheet, total current assets were $4,524,021, and total current liabilities were $2,413,867, a ratio of approximately 1.9 to 1. This was bad enough, but on the true facts, the ratio was worse. As corrected, current assets, as near as one can tell, were approximately $3,924,000, and current liabilities approximately $2,478,000, a ratio of approximately 1.6 to 1.

Would it have made any difference if a prospective purchaser of these debentures had been advised of these facts? There must be some point at which errors in disclosing a company's balance sheet position

---

[3]This figure assumes that the entire $264,689 of factors' reserves was noncurrent. Some part of it probably was current on the theory that part would be released by the factors within one year, but this amount cannot be determined on the evidence and, in any case, it would seem to have been small.

become material, even to a growth-oriented investor. On all the evidence I find that these balance sheet errors were material within the meaning of Section 11.

Since there was an abundance of material misstatements pertaining to 1961 affairs, whether or not the errors in the 1960 figures were material does not affect the outcome of this case except to the extent that it bears upon the liability of Peat, Marwick. That subject will be discussed hereinafter.

The "Due Diligence" Defenses

Section 11(b) of the Act provides that:

". . . no person, other than the issuer, shall be liable . . . who shall sustain the burden of proof —

* * *

(3) that (A) as regards any part of the registration statement not purporting to be made on the authority of an expert . . . he had, after reasonable investigation, reasonable ground to believe and did believe, at the time such part of the registration statement became effective, that the statements therein were true and that there was no omission to state a material fact required to be stated therein or necessary to make the statements therein not misleading; . . . and (C) as regards any part of the registration statement purporting to be made on the authority of an expert (other than himself) . . . he had no reasonable ground to believe and did not believe, at the time such part of the registration statement became effective, that the statements therein were untrue or that there was an omission to state a material fact required to be stated therein or necessary to make the statements therein not misleading . . . ."

Section 11(c) defines "reasonable investigation" as follows:

"In determining, for the purpose of paragraph (3) of subsection (b) of this section, what constitutes reasonable investigation and reasonable ground for belief, the standard of reasonableness shall be that required of a prudent man in the management of his own property."

Every defendant, except BarChris itself, to whom, as the issuer, these defenses are not available, and except Peat, Marwick, whose position rests on a different statutory provision,[4] has pleaded these

---

[4]This statutory provision will be quoted in discussing Peat, Marwick's liability *infra.*

affirmative defenses. Each claims that (1) as to the part of the registration statement purporting to be made on the authority of an expert (which, for convenience, I shall refer to as the "expertised portion"), he had no reasonable ground to believe and did not believe that there were any untrue statements or material omissions, and (2) as to the other parts of the registration statement, he made a reasonable investigation, as a result of which he had reasonable ground to believe and did believe that the registration statement was true and that no material fact was omitted. As to each defendant, the question is whether he has sustained the burden of proving these defenses. Surprising enough, there is little or no judicial authority on this question. No decisions directly in point under Section 11 have been found.

Before considering the evidence, a preliminary matter should be disposed of. The defendants do not agree among themselves as to who the "experts" were or as to the parts of the registration statement which were expertised. Some defendants say that Peat, Marwick was the expert, others say that BarChris' attorneys, Perkins, Daniels, McCormack & Collins, and the underwriters' attorneys, Drinker, Biddle & Reath, were also the experts. On the first view, only those portions of the registration statement purporting to be made on Peat, Marwick's authority were expertised portions. On the other view everything in the registration statement was within this category, because the two law firms were responsible for the entire document.

The first view is the correct one. To say that the entire registration statement is expertised because some lawyer prepared it would be an unreasonable construction of the statute. Neither the lawyer for the company nor the lawyer for the underwriters is an expert within the meaning of Section 11. The only expert, in the statutory sense, was Peat, Marwick, and the only parts of the registration statement which purported to be made upon the authority of an expert were the portions which purported to be made on Peat, Marwick's authority.

The parties also disagree as to what those portions were. Some defendants say that it was only the 1960 figures (and the figures for prior years, which are not in controversy here). Others say in substance that it was every figure in the prospectus. The plaintiffs take a somewhat intermediate view. They do not claim that Peat, Marwick expertised every figure, but they do maintain that Peat, Marwick is responsible for a portion of the text of the prospectus, *i.e.,* that pertaining to "Methods of Operation," because a reference to it was made in footnote 9 to the balance sheet.

Here again, the more narrow view is the correct one. The registration statement contains a report of Peat, Marwick as independent public accountants dated February 23, 1961. This relates only to the consolidated balance sheet of BarChris and consolidated subsidiaries as of December 31, 1960, and the related statement of earnings and retained earnings for the five years then ended. This is all that Peat, Marwick purported to certify. It is perfectly clear that it did not purport to certify the 1961 figures, some of which are expressly stated in the prospectus to have been unaudited.

Moreover, plaintiffs' intermediate view is also incorrect. The cross reference in footnote 9 to the "Methods of Operation" passage in the prospectus was inserted merely for the convenience of the reader. It is not a fair construction to say that it thereby imported into the balance sheet everything in that portion of the text, much of which had nothing to do with the figures in the balance sheet.

I turn now to the question of whether defendants have proved their due diligence defenses. The position of each defendant will be separately considered.

* * *

Peat, Marwick

Section 11(b) provides:

"Notwithstanding the provisions of subsection (a) no person . . . shall be liable as provided therein who shall sustain the burden of proof —
* * *

"(3) that . . . (B) as regards any part of the registration statement purporting to be made upon his authority as an expert . . . (i) he had, after reasonable investigation, reasonable ground to believe and did believe, at the time such part of the registration statement became effective, that the statements therein were true and that there was no omission to state a material fact required to be stated therein or necessary to make the statements therein not misleading . . . ."

This defines the due diligence defense for an expert. Peat, Marwick has pleaded it.

The part of the registration statement purporting to be made upon the authority of Peat, Marwick as an expert was, as we have seen, the 1960 figures. But because the statute requires the court to determine Peat, Marwick's belief, and the grounds thereof, "at the time such part of the registration statement became effective," for the purposes of this affirmative defense the matter must be viewed as of May 16, 1961, and the question is whether at that time Peat, Marwick, after reasonable investigation, had reasonable ground to believe and did believe that the 1960 figures were true and that no material fact had been omitted from the registration statement which should have been included in order to make the 1960 figures not misleading. In deciding this issue, the court must consider not only what Peat, Marwick did in its 1960 audit, but also what it did in its subsequent "S-1 review." The proper scope of that review must also be determined.

It may be noted that we are concerned at this point only with the question of Peat, Marwick's liability to plantiffs. At the closing on May 24, 1961, Peat, Marwick delivered a so-called "comfort letter" to the underwriters. This letter stated:

"It is understood that this letter is for the information of the underwriters and is not to be quoted or referred to, in whole or in part, in the Registration Statement or Prospectus or in any literature used in connection with the sale of securities."

Plaintiffs may not take advantage of any undertakings or representations in this letter. If they exceeded the normal scope of an S-1 review (a question which I do not now decide), that is a matter which relates only to the crossclaims which defendants have asserted against each other and which I have postponed for determination at a later date.

The 1960 Audit

Peat, Marwick's work was in general charge of a member of the firm, Cummings, and more immediately in charge of Peat, Marwick's manager, Logan. Most of the actual work was performed by a senior accountant, Berardi, who had junior assistants, one of whom was Kennedy.

Berardi was then about thirty years old. He was not yet a C.P.A. He had had no previous experience with the bowling industry. This was his first job as a senior accountant. He could hardly have been given a more difficult assignment.

After obtaining a little background information on BarChris by talking to Logan and reviewing Peat, Marwick's work papers on its 1959 audit, Berardi examined the results of test checks of BarChris' accounting procedures which one of the junior accountants had made, and he prepared an "internal control questionnaire" and an "audit program." Thereafter, for a few days subsequent to December 30, 1960, he inspected BarChris' inventories and examined certain alley construction. Finally, on January 13, 1961, he began his auditing work which he carried on substantially continuously until it was completed on February 24, 1961. Toward the close of the work, Logan reviewed it and made various comments and suggestions to Berardi.

It is unnecessary to recount everything that Berardi did in the course of the audit. We are concerned only with the evidence relating to what Berardi did or did not do with respect to those items which I have found to have been incorrectly reported in the 1960 figures in the prospectus. More narrowly, we are directly concerned only with such of those items as I have found to be material.

Capitol Lanes

First and foremost is Berardi's failure to discover that Capitol Lanes had not been sold. This error affected both the sales figure and the liability side of the balance sheet. Fundamentally, the error stemmed from the fact that Berardi never realized that Heavenly Lanes and Capitol were two different names for the same alley. In the course of his audit, Berardi was shown BarChris's contract file. He examined the contracts in the file and made a list of them. The file must have included a contract with an outside purchaser for Heavenly Lanes, although no such contract was ever produced at the trial, for Berardi included Heavenly on his list. Apparently there was no contract in the file for a lane named Capitol because that name did not appear on Berardi's list.

Kircher also made a list of jobs. Heavenly was on his list. Capitol was not. Berardi compared the two lists and satisfied himself that he had the proper jobs to be taken into account. Berardi assumed that Heavenly was to be treated like any other completed job. He included it in all his computations.

The evidence is conflicting as to whether BarChris' officers expressly informed Berardi that Heavenly and Capitol were the same thing and that BarChris was operating Capitol and had not sold it. I find that they did not so inform him.

Berardi did become aware that there were references here and there in BarChris' records to something called Capitol Lanes. He also knew that there were indications that at some time BarChris might operate an alley of that name. He read the minutes of the board of directors' meeting of November 22, 1960 which recited that:

". . . the Chairman recommended that the Corporation operate Capitol Lanes, 271 Main Street, East Haven, Connecticut, through a corporation which would be a subsidiary of Sanpark Realty Corp."

The minutes further recorded that:

". . . it was unanimously agreed that the officers of the Corporation exercise their discretion as to operating Capitol Lanes through the aforesaid subsidiary on an experimental basis."

The junior accountant, Kennedy, read the minute book of Capitol Lanes, Inc., a Connecticut corporation organized in December 1960. The book contained a certificate of incorporation which empowered the corporation, among many other things, to own and manage bowling alleys. There was no minutes in the book, however, that indicated that the corporation actually did own or manage one.

Berardi knew from various BarChris records that Capitol Lanes, Inc. was paying rentals to Talcott. Also, a Peat, Marwick work paper bearing Kennedy's initials recorded that Capitol Lanes, Inc. held certain insurance policies, including a fire insurance policy on "contents," a workman's compensation and a public liability policy. Another Peat, Marwick work paper also bearing Kennedy's initials recorded that Capitol Lanes, Inc. had $1,000 in a fund in Connecticut. A note on this paper read:

"Traced to disbursements book — advanced for operation of alley — not expensed at 12/31/60."

Logan's written comments upon the audit contained an entry reading as follows:

"When talking to Ted Kircher in latter part of '60 he indicated one subsidiary is leasing alley built by BarChris — the profit on this job should be eliminated as its ownership is within the affiliated group."

Opposite this note is an entry by Berardi reading as follows:

"Properties sold to others by affiliates. Capitol Lanes is paying currently lease rentals which amount to a lease purchase plan."

This note is somewhat ambiguous. If by "others" Berardi meant outside buyers, then it would seem that he should have accounted in some way for this sale, which he did not do. Presumably, by "others" he meant "other affiliates." Hence, he regarded the transaction, whatever he thought it to have been, as an intercompany one. Apparently Logan so understood Berardi's explanation.

Berardi testified that he inquired of Russo about Capitol Lanes and that Russo told him that Capitol Lanes, Inc., was going to operate an alley some day but as yet it had no alley. Berardi testified that he understood that the alley had not been built and that he believed that the rental payments were on vacant land.

I am not satisfied with this testimony. If Berardi did hold this belief, he should not have held it. The entries as to insurance and as to "operation of alley" should have alerted him to the fact that an alley existed. He should have made further inquiry on the subject. It is apparent that Berardi did not understand this transaction.

In any case, he never identified this mysterious Capitol with the Heavenly Lanes which he had included in his sales and profit figures. The vital question is whether he failed to make a reasonable investigation which, if he had made it, would have revealed the truth.

Certain accounting records of BarChris, which Berardi testified he did not see, would have put him on inquiry. One was a job cost ledger card for job no. 6036, the job number which Berardi put on his own sheet for Heavenly Lanes. This card read "Capitol Theatre (Heavenly)." In addition, two accounts receivable cards each showed both names on the same card, Capitol and Heavenly. Berardi testified that he looked at the accounts receivable records but that he did not see these particular cards. He testified that he did not look on the job cost ledger cards because he took the costs from another record, the costs register.

The burden of proof on this issue is on Peat, Marwick. Although the question is a rather close one, I find that Peat, Marwick has not sustained that burden. Peat, Marwick has not proved that Berardi made a reasonable investigation as far as Capitol Lanes was concerned and that his ignorance of the true facts was justified.

Howard Lanes Annex

Berardi also failed to discover that this alley was not sold. Here the evidence is much scantier. Berardi saw a contract for this alley in the contract file. No one told him that it was to be leased rather than sold. There is no evidence to indicate that any record existed which would have put him on notice. I find that his investigation was reasonable as to this item.

Burke Lanes

This $25,000 error was not material. Furthermore, there is nothing to show that it was Berardi's fault. He was advised that the item represented "extra work." He had no reasonable ground to believe that actually it was a loan.

Worcester and Atlas-Bedford

I have already found that Berardi erred in treating these two alleys as fully completed and that he should have taken Pugliese's estimate. I have also found, however, that this error was not material.

This disposes of the inaccuracies in the 1960 sales figures. I turn now to the errors in the current assets which involve four items: cash, reserve for Federal Lanes, factors' reserves and Howard Lanes Annex, which latter I have already covered.

As to cash, Berardi properly obtained a confirmation from the bank as to BarChris' cash balance on December 31, 1960. He did not know that part of this balance had been temporarily increased by the deposit of reserves returned by Talcott to BarChris conditionally for a limited time. I do not believe that Berardi reasonably should have known this. Although Peat, Marwick's work papers record the fact that these reserves were returned, there was nothing to indicate that the payment was conditional. Russo obviously did not reveal this fact. It would not be reasonable to require Berardi to examine all of Bar-Chris' correspondence files when he had no reason to suspect any irregularity.

As to the reserve on Federal Lanes, there is little to add to the earlier discussion of this subject in this opinion. I appreciate that in that instance the court has substituted its judgment for that of Russo and Berardi. For the reasons previously mentioned, I believe that their judgment was clearly wrong.

As to factors' reserves, it is hard to understand how Berardi could have treated this item as entirely a current asset when it was obvious that most of the reserves would not be released within one year. If Berardi was unaware of that fact, he should have been aware of it.

The net result, as far as current assets are concerned, is that Peat, Marwick is responsible for the errors as to reserves but not for those involving the cash item and the receivable from Howard Lanes Annex.

Contingent Liabilities

Berardi erred in computing the contingent liability on Type B leaseback transaction at 25 percent. He testified that he was shown an agreement with Talcott which fixed the contingent liability at that amount. In this testimony he was mistaken. No such document is contained in Peat, Marwick's work papers. The evidence indicates that it never existed. Berardi did not examine the documents which are in evidence which establish that BarChris' contingent liability on this type of transaction was in fact 100 percent. Berardi did make a reasonable investigation in this instance. Although I have found that the error in understating contingent liabilities as of December 31, 1960 would not have deterred a prospective purchaser, the error is nevertheless of some importance because it apparently led Trilling into making a larger error in computing the contingent liability figure as of April 30, 1961.

The S-1 Review

The purpose of reviewing events subsequent to the date of a certified balance sheet (referred to as an S-1 review when made with reference to a registration statement) is to ascertain whether any material change has occurred in the company's financial position which should be disclosed in order to prevent the balance sheet figures from being misleading. The scope of such a review, under generally accepted auditing standards, is limited. It does not amount to a complete audit.

Peat, Marwick prepared a written program for such a review. I find that this program conformed to generally accepted auditing standards. Among other things, it required the following:

"1. Review minutes of stockholders, directors and committees . . . .

"2. Review latest interim financial statements and compare with corresponding statements of preceding year. Inquire regarding significant variations and changes.

* * *

"4. Review the more important financial records and inquire regarding material transactions not in the ordinary course of business and any other significant items.

* * *

"6. Inquire as to changes in material contracts . . . .

* * *

"10. Inquire as to any significant bad debts or accounts in dispute for which provision has not been made.

* * *

"14. Inquire as to . . . newly discovered liabilities, direct or contingent. . . ."

Berardi made the S-1 review in May 1961. He devoted a little over two days to it, a total of 20½ hours. He did not discover any of the errors or omissions pertaining to the state of affairs in 1961 which I have previously discussed at length, all of which were material. The question is whether, despite his failure to find out anything, his investigation was reasonable within the meaning of the statute.

What Berardi did was to look at a consolidating trial balance as of March 31, 1961 which had been prepared by BarChris, compare it with the audited December 31, 1960 figures, discuss with Trilling certain unfavorable developments which the comparison disclosed, and read certain minutes. He did not examine any "important financial records" other than the trial balance. As to minutes, he read only what minutes Birnbaum gave him, which consisted only of the board of directors' minutes of BarChris. He did not read such minutes as there were of the executive committee. He did not know that there was an executive committee, hence he did not discover that Kircher had notes of executive committee minutes which had not been written up. He did not read the minutes of any subsidiary.

In substance, what Berardi did is similar to what Grant and Ballard did. He asked questions, he got answers which he considered satisfactory, and he did nothing to verify them. For example, he obtained from Trilling a list of contracts. The list included Yonkers and Bridge. Since Berardi did not read the minutes of subsidiaries, he did not learn that Yonkers and Bridge were intercompany sales. The list also included Woonsocket and the six T-Bowl jobs, Moravia Road, Milford, Groton, North Attleboro, Odenton and Severna Park. Since Berardi did not look at any contract documents, and since he was unaware of the executive committee minutes of March 18, 1961 (at that time embodied only in Kircher's notes), he did not learn that BarChris had no contracts for these jobs. Trilling's list did not set forth contract prices for them, although it did for Yonkers, Bridge and certain others. This did not arouse Berardi's suspicion.

Berardi noticed that there had been an increase in notes payable by BarChris. Trilling admitted to him that BarChris was "a bit slow" in paying its bills. Berardi recorded in his notes of his review that Bar-Chris was in a "tight cash position." Trilling's explanation was that BarChris was experiencing "some temporary difficulty."

Berardi had no conception of how tight the cash position was. He did not discover that BarChris was holding up checks in substantial amounts because there was no money in the bank to cover them.[5] He did not know of the loan from Manufacturers Trust Company or of the officers' loans. Since he never read the prospectus, he was not even aware that there had ever been any problem about loans from officers.

During the 1960 audit Berardi had obtained some information from factors, not sufficiently detailed even then, as to delinquent notes. He made no inquiry of factors about this in his S-1 review. Since he knew nothing about Kircher's notes of the executive committee meetings, he did not learn that the delinquency situation had grown worse. He was content with Trilling's assurance that no liability theretofore contingent had become direct.

Apparently the only BarChris officer with whom Berardi communicated was Trilling. He could not recall making any inquiries of Russo, Vitolo or Pugliese. As to Kircher, Berardi's testimony was self-contradictory. At one point he said that he had inquired of Kircher and at another he said that he could not recall making any such inquiry.

There had been a material change for the worse in BarChris' financial position. That change was sufficiently serious so that the failure to disclose it made the 1960 figures misleading. Berardi did not discover it. As far as results were concerned, his S-1 review was useless.

Accountants should not be held to a standard higher than that recognized in their profession. I do not do so here. Berardi's review did not come up to that standard. He did not take some of the steps

---

[5]One of these checks was a check to the order of Peat, Marwick in the amount of $3,000. It was dated April 4, 1961. It was deposited by Peat, Marwick on May 29, 1961.

which Peat, Marwick's written program prescribed. He did not spend an adequate amount of time on a task of this magnitude. Most important of all, he was too easily satisfied with glib answers to his inquiries.

This is not to say that he should have made a complete audit. But there were enough danger signals in the materials which he did examine to require some further investigation on his part. Generally accepted accounting standards required such further investigation under these circumstances. It is not always sufficient merely to ask questions.

Here again, the burden of proof is on Peat, Marwick. I find that that burden has not been satisfied. I conclude that Peat, Marwick has not established its due diligence defense.

* * *

Issues for consideration:

(1) What do you consider the *basic* deficiencies, if any, in the auditors':
   a. Auditing procedures, including the "subsequent review," and
   b. Report on the financial statements?

(2) The court stated that "Accountants should not be held to a standard higher than that recognized in their profession." Compare this point of view with the position taken by the court in the Continental Vending Corporation case.

(3) Why did the court find a 16% overstatement of working capital to be material whereas it did not find a 14% overstatement of earnings per share to be material?

(4) What are some important lessons to be learned by the accounting profession from the BarChris decision?